Man Of The Sahara

A Long Walk To Tuareg Statehood

by Akli Sh'kka

"60 years of violent conflict, and resistance."

Published by New Generation Publishing in 2020

First Edition

ISBN
      Paperback   978-1-80031-467-2
      Hardback   978-1-80031-466-5

www.newgeneration-publishing.com

New Generation Publishing

Acknowledgement

My completion of this book could not have been accomplished without the support and help of my friends, Sharoun, Eve, Barbara and John. Thank you all. You deserve a trip to Tenere!

Contents

Map of Azawad 1

Introduction 3

Chapter 1: Speaking to the United Nations in 2016..........4

Chapter 2: Terrorism and the Indigenous Tuaregs............9

Chapter 3: Hope for an Independent Azawad 17

Chapter 4: The Legacy of French Neo-Colonialism 24

Photographs...30

Chapter 5: Conflicting Divisions in the tuareg Liberation
Movements...36

Chapter 6: Resistance from Ethnic Groups in Mali 45

Chapter 7: The Role of Neighbouring States in the Failure
of Azawad 52

Chapter 8: The 2020 Coup D'Etat and Demoncratic Sham
in Mali 60

Photographs...68

Chapter 9: Compairing the Tuaregs in Mali with Those
Elsewhere 80

Chapter 10: The Effect of the Algiers 2015 Peace Accords
....92

Chapter 11: Toumast and the Influence of the Media on
our Independence 96

Chapter 12: Looking to the Future of Azawad...............105

Author's Note 111

This book is dedicated to the memory of those Tuaregs who have died in the Sahara because of conflict and violence. And all others who still keep the hope for peace in their hearts.

A percentage of the proceeds of sale from this book will be used to build schools in the region, and promote other peaceful purposes.

Map of Azawad

Introduction

My name is Akli Sh'kka. I wrote this book to tell you the story of an ancient people. Their Sons, and Daughters. The land they also loved, and their animals.

How they were free to go where their Fathers, and Fathers before them, had walked for thousands of years. The beautiful Tifinagh script they used. Traditional proverbs; poetry, and song. Theirs was a distinctive way of life which enabled them to control the caravan trading routes across the desert, and found the ancient city of Tinbuktu which you may know now as Timbuktu.

But all of this changed historically, once colonisation and global politics intervened. More recently, through the rise of political Islam; jihadism, and terrorism. Whilst successive governments in Mali and its neighbouring countries became corrupt. So that many living there have been forced into poverty. Often without food; adequate shelter, or medicine.

A proud and noble people who still dream of a better life for their families, and themselves. Of a place called Azawad, the independent state where they could have left behind the horror of war; violation of human rights, and degradation from which they are suffering. Allowing them not only to survive, but to live in peace.

This is the story of the Tuaregs, a nomadic tribe and nation of Africa, who lived on the sands of the Sahara for as long as men and women have had memory. ...I am a Tuareg, so this is also my story.

Chapter 1

Speaking To The United Nations In 2016

I was invited to speak to the United Nations, Permanent Forum in Indigenous Issues, during 2016 about what had happened to the Tuareg people. The conflict they continued to face, and the possibilities for peace. How they might be recognised again as a nation, as well as the urgent help they needed to put a stop to the violation of their human rights. My speech was made that day to the people of the world, through the United Nations' representatives. Whom I still regard as my brothers; sisters, and friends.

I made this speech on behalf of the nomadic Tuaregs of the Sahara, and more specifically, a non-government organisation called The Imouhagh International Organisation for Justice and Transparency. I explained that my concern for the future of the Tuareg people came from at least one hundred and eighty years of unspeakable persecution, and maltreatment which still continues today. Just as I will tell you in this book, the Tuareg traditional lands known as the Tenere in our language, being historically divided up into new states by Italian and French colonial governments.

The Human Rights violations committed against the Tuareg people include mass killings, and a long list of other horrific atrocities. Individual stories of forced conscription into the army and militia; heavy militarisation of huge areas; destruction of our cultural heritage; the immigrant settlement of confiscated territories, and the displacement of people through the deprivation of their livelihood. Too many of these situations have sadly been unreported, and continue to this day to be ignored by the mainstream media.

The people whom this has affected have been pushed into what may be described as, political invisibility. During 2014 and 2015, the Tuaregs experienced a particularly shocking violation of their human rights, that also breached international humanitarian laws. As well as being defined as criminal activity, perpetrated by different states.

I went on to explain to the United Nations how the Tuaregs had struggled for freedom with successive governments of Mali, and to regain their right to self-governance. Since its creation as a new and independent state in 1960. The subsequent demarcation of new borders at that time had left the Tuareg people without a land to call their own. Despite the fact that we were the original inhabitants of the area. All of this was completely ignored. Our ancient and traditional lands were from our point of view randomly divided between four artificially created countries. Libya; Algeria; Niger, and Mali.

This enormous damage to the fabric of Tuareg society naturally led to conflict. It also put an end to the possibility of a peaceful co-existence for the people in this part of the Sahara. 2012 was one of the worst years in living memory for war crimes perpetrated against the Tuareg people. Crimes committed not only in Mali, but throughout the whole region. On February 22nd a decision was made by elements of the Malian army to avenge various attacks; war crimes, and other abuses. All of which had been committed earlier by the soldiers in that same Malian Army and its militias, in particular the Ganda Koy. Whilst between May 2015 and March 2016, one hundred and seventy civilians were killed, again by the Malian army; its militias, and related terrorist groups. The perpetrators have still not been brought to justice.

Life for the Tuareg population in Libya took a turn for the worse during the fall of the Qaddafi regime. Hundreds of Tuaregs were arrested; tortured, and killed. Others were imprisoned once they had been identified. This happened in Tripoli; Misrata; and El Zawiya, as well as elsewhere in the country. In Ghadames on May 19th, 2012 further war crimes were committed by the militias. These were supported and financed by the Libyan Interior Minister, Nasser Almanae, who was also from Ghadames. Twenty innocent, unarmed, men were assassinated. Thirty three houses belonging to Tuareg people were also demolished, by levelling them to the ground. While other members of the militia burned their animals, and it didn't stop there. The Tuaregs' ancient heritage buildings were also demolished, and their cultural artefacts destroyed.

Another incident occurred further south in Oubari on September 17th, 2015. When an alliance of ideologically armed tribes and militias launched a series of attacks against the Tuareg people. Killing dozens of innocent, unarmed, civilians. Hundreds of houses in Oubari and Sebha were again destroyed by armed groups. Using bulldozers; heavy weapons, and grenades. All of which belonged to the Tuaregs.

And yet again, twenty three thousand Tuareg people in Libya had been denied Libyan nationality and normal identity documents. Their children had been deprived of schooling, because of not having a so-called national number, or identity papers.

Whilst the situation of the Tuareg in Algeria can only be described as disastrous. Dozens of them have been arrested, and detained without trial. Simply because of their ethnic identity. Most of the detainees were nomads, or cattle herders. Neither family members nor close friends were allowed to visit them. The prisoners also didn't have access to legal aid.

On April 4th, 2016 the Algerian authorities demolished one hundred houses in Tamanrasset in the far south, without giving prior notice of their intention to do so. They have still not provided a copy, or shown evidence that it exists, of the decision to knock down these Tuareg houses with the occupants inside them. Four women suffered aborted pregnancies because of the trauma they suffered that day, and fourteen peaceful protesters were put in jail. More than one hundred families became homeless that day, without any alternative shelter or assistance being given by the government.

I told the United Nations that Niger was not meeting the genuine requirements of its indigenous people, especially in relation to land and the environment. This could be seen quite clearly from Greenpeace, and other human rights reports at that time. The Tuareg rebellion of 2009 had culminated in a peace agreement between the Tuareg rebels and Nigerian officials, but only a small part of this agreement had been implemented. Again, despite the Nigerian governmental army having committed massacres and war crimes during the 1990s and in 2008, the perpetrators had still not been brought to justice.

A Greenpeace report in 2010, and other reliable accounts, indicated that as many as hundreds of Tuareg nomads had died as a result of Areva's operations in the area. The French nuclear giant produced uranium and chemical materials in Arlit; Akokan village, and elsewhere in the region. So that the people from there had for the first time in Tuareg history experienced "unusual" diseases. All of which followed Areva's arrival, during 1970. Helping France enjoy nuclear power for three quarters of its electricity, and making it more reliant on uranium than any other country. The reality was that whilst Paris enjoyed light and clean water, Tuareg children and adult nomads were dying of extreme hunger and pollution. Radioactivity which caused respiratory problems; birth defects; leukemia, and cancer.

I told the United Nations that day I wished only to stress the following:

Firstly that the indigenous people of the Sahara, the Tuaregs, could happily and usefully play an important role in any attempt to bring peace and stability to the region. If only they were given sufficient trust, by the governments of the different states in the region, to enable them to do so.

Secondly, the countries concerned must no longer be allowed to get away with these human rights' violations, without any proper punishment or sanctions being applied.

Thirdly, I asked the United Nations to put more pressure on its member states in the Sahara region. With a view to ending discrimination; marginalisation, and persecution of the Tuareg people. In a territory that must be recognised as having been theirs, for many thousands of years.

Finally, it was necessary to recognise universally that all Tuaregs had a right to a nationality. The documentation of an identity that accompanies this should be granted to the Tuareg people of Libya without further delay, pursuant to the United Nations Declaration on the Rights of Indigenous Peoples.

This is what I told the United Nations in 2016, and four years later, so much of it still remains to be done.

Chapter 2

Terrorism And The Indigenous Tuaregs

What I have described in Chapter 1 are not the only reasons why my people, the Tuaregs, are continuing to suffer and we can no longer regard ourselves as a unified nation. I was also invited to New York in 2016, to speak at the Fifth Biennial SUNY Binghamton Graduate Conference on World History And Social Science. I talked on this occasion about how Islamic extremists were threatening our culture, and traditional way of life. In the Sahara where many still lived, albeit in diminishing numbers. Whether they remained nomadic or had become temporarily settled, a number of terrorist organisations had also appeared on the scene. Driven by distorted, fundamentalist, ideas or ideologies which had been successfully propagated. These were also being used by corrupt government officials to further their own self interest.

It had become a terrorism which threatened any real prospect of future peace; security, and human rights in this region. Hundreds of uneducated and jobless young Tuaregs, as well as youngsters from other ethnicities, had been drawn into well-funded terrorist groups. More and more recruits were being attracted to them day after day, because of the fundamentalists' clever use of social media, in an age when smartphones and tablets had rapidly become commonplace almost everywhere.

I told the Conference that I believed a major cause of this flow of young and naive "cannon fodder" was the absence of any regular source of a strong counter-narrative which they could listen to. There was still a very great need for a competent, and lively source of good information. One that was independent; reliable, and persuasive. Also communicating with young people in their own native language. Establishing such an enterprise, a really good one and which was my personal ambition, would be the most promising way to combat all the misinformation currently being fed to them. The flawed logic of these missionaries of unreason who dominated the various networks, and airwaves. Many hardliners had been misusing the good name of Islam, to spread deplorable misinterpretations of scripture and other deeply questionable ideas, amongst the Tuareg nomads. A people who were previously essentially moderate, and peace loving.

I went on to say that there really was nothing out there, to enlighten the young and naive Tuaregs, regarding the true nature and identity of the "bad guys" seeking to bring them on board. A means was urgently needed to help explain the corrupt nature, and likely consequences, of their deplorable actions and activities which were quite clearly doomed. Whatever damage they managed to do in the meantime. Also, to make apparent the insanity behind these ideas. Whatever the immediate appeal might be of the highly visible, even heroic aspect, of this frequent immolation and self-sacrifice. Which often strongly appealed to rebels without a cause who felt deprived; frustrated, and unhappy. Making them ripe material for such ruthless indoctrination.

The absence of any quality media, with interesting programmes and reasonable messages put across persuasively, had made it all too easy for extremists to spread their toxic madness. Terrorism and Islamic extremism were flourishing throughout large parts of this vast territory. For the first time in the Sahara, a number of fundamentalist groups with highly dangerous ideologies and inflexible doctrines, were steadily expanding their influence among the ancient people of the desert.

The Tuaregs have been thought for a long time to be relatively moderate in their beliefs, and practice as Muslims. Which has for centuries made co-existence with more fervent groups quite difficult. Because the Tuaregs are often seen as imperfect Muslims, they have on occasions been called infidels. Especially regarding the position of women in our society. Where the relative freedom of every female is part of a long established tradition. Historically, ours is essentially a matriarchal society in which monogamy is the rule. It is unusual for us to have more than one spouse. So just as with other nomadic groups or tribes, the Tuaregs have often been perceived as an objectionable threat by others. Those who have a blinkered or intolerant outlook see them as a threat, to the pure belief system which they follow.

We know from archaeologists and historians that Tuareg nomads were almost certainly the first humans to appear in North Africa in the area that is now called the Sahara Desert, at least three thousand years ago. Whilst in our own language the Sahara is called the Tenere. A word that can also mean nostalgia; isolation, or loneliness. A perfect description of it. For the purposes of this book I have used the name "Tuareg" in categorising others, and myself. However, we don't usually refer to ourselves by this word. We prefer instead to be known as Kel Tamacheq; Kel Tamajeght; Imushagh, or Imuhagh. These words mean: free men. As well as nobles, and speakers of Tamacheqt. A language also known as Tamazight and, more familiarly in the west, Berber.

You may also have heard the name Kel Tagelmust being used. This means the people of the veil, or blue men. Until the 1960s the Tuaregs' livelihood was mostly based on their animals. They were traders dealing in dates, and slabs of salt. A major source of which was a remote place called

Taoudenni. More than six hundred and fifty kilometers north of Tinbuktu where they could extract this from an ancient salt lake. In exchange for salt and dates, they would receive food and clothes at a number of places to meet their basic requirements. These are now known as Niger; Mali; Burkina Faso, and Senegal.

At the turn of the nineteenth century, the Tuareg territory was organised into confederations. Each of which was ruled by a supreme chief or Amenokal, who worked with a council of elders drawn from different tribes. These confederations are still sometimes called Atabel which means drum groups in our native language. After the drum which was the Amenokal's symbol of authority. The clan elders, known as the Imgharen or wise men, were chosen to assist the chief of the confederation. There were seven recent major confederations. Namely Kel Ajjer (located in southern Libya); Kel Ahaggar (in southern Algeria); Kel Adagh (northern Mali); Kel Air (northern Niger) and Kel Azawagh (western Niger).

As I mentioned in chapter 1, the Tuareg nation was divided by artificial frontiers drawn on a map in Paris during the early 1960s. Being split between five countries, the successors to former French colonies in north and west Africa. Namely Mali; Burkina Faso; Niger; Libya; Algeria, and Morocco. As a result, what had once been a single tribe or nation, for as long as we know, was divided up by completely arbitrary and imaginary frontiers. Planned, and decided, by French colonial authorities. With no account being taken of the social fabric, or relationships and ties of the inhabitants, the so-called Tuareg people whose roots run deep within the Tenere.

Before the imposition of these lines, deemed to be appropriate as international frontiers and boundaries, the Sahara was under Tuareg authority. It was one of the safest, and most beautiful places in the world. As soon as this power was taken from us and given to others, problems very quickly began to arise. In relation to the main routes that connected the north west and north of Africa (Morocco; Algeria, and Libya) with places to the south and west of the Sahara (Niger; Mali; Chad, and Senegal) it used to be said that: "even a tiny fly could not cross the Sahara without the permission of the Tuaregs!" Such was the extent of our control, and respect, for the land we loved.

I told the Graduate Conference in 2016 that this image of our traditional homeland, and saying, was no longer heard. People talked about other things instead that concerned them more; frightened, or worried them. Like corruption within their governments; terrorism; kidnapping; human trafficking, and illegal immigration. Things which until a little while ago had been totally alien to the Tuareg culture. They simply did not exist in our society.

All of this did of course mean that our Tuareg culture and traditions were in grave danger of not surviving. Mostly because of corruption and the new waves of extremism the Sahara had witnessed over the last few years. Such as those seen in Tinbuktu during 2012. Whole areas; valleys; villages, and other places that had long established names in the Tuareg language had since then been re-named by national authorities. They still remain subject to change in other African languages, and Arabic.

In school textbooks you will rarely find any mention of my people's history, or famous leaders. Like Hannibal, and Tarek Ben Ziyad. Both of whom are incorrectly referred to now as Arabs! Whilst the Tenere has become dangerous because of illegal migration; mineral exploitation; terrorist groups, and there being only a few of the last remaining nomads in evidence. Those fellow human beings who had skilfully lived an extraordinary life close to nature for thousands of years, and maybe longer. I told the conference that it seemed incredible something like this was being allowed to happen in the twenty-first century.

Even more so perhaps, given the history of my people? For many centuries, a variety of invaders with different belief systems and strong religious ideas, had encountered the nomadic Tuareg. As they roamed their homeland, or settled in an oasis. None of these newcomers was however able to defeat, and subsequently rule our independent nation. Nor greatly change, never mind erase, its cultural heritage of ancient belief and customs. Throughout the history of Islam in northern Africa, the Tuareg people avoided engaging in wars against the Muslims, Messengers of Allah. In the same way as we courteously welcomed other religions, including Judaism and Christianity, we did not automatically resist or fight those who came later with their Islamic religious messages. When armed resistance did occur from time to time, this was usually because of the newcomers' refusal to respect our age-old traditions. One of which in particular was the position of women in Tuareg society. That they should be treated as equal to men. Something which has always been considered unnegotiable, even sacrosanct, by us.

Consequently, the Tuareg people earned a reputation amongst the north African Arabs as being lax about common Islamic practices. In fact, you could even say that they had shaped their own religious beliefs. They had developed unique cultural practices concerning Islam. Even though they remained part of the overall totality, or "club" of Islamic African nations. A good example of this is when women are not required to practise chastity before marriage.

Long before Judaism; Christianity, or Islam came into existence the Tuareg people worshiped Tannit. The Goddess of rain who was also a fertility symbol. This may be where the role and position which Tuareg women enjoy today originated. As we still think of a woman as being divine. Even though she was born a human being. Tuareg society also has other particular practises, and beliefs. The very different position of a Tuareg woman is clearly demonstrated again in the traditional blue veil. This is worn by their men, not them. The men wear a turban; veil, or headdress in part. As a symbolic protection against evil spirits and the desert's cruel nature. They usually start wearing this when they are recognised as young or *Amaouad* adults at the age of sixteen, and continue to do so until death.

A stark contrast to the traditional Islamic practice in which females are obliged to wear a headscarf, or veil. Allegedly to protect their modesty. Although this assertion has been criticised by feminist groups. They have questioned whether there are other forces at work responsible for this, apart from the requirements of the Qur'an. Given its occurrence in a male led, and male dominated culture. Whilst the desert nomads developed a version of Islam which was well suited to their way of life. We have long practiced a Sunni version of Islam, with some variation. Perhaps the greatest area of difference lies in the most fundamental object or concept of this religion? Namely, the focus or object of our worship.

Islam teaches belief in a monotheistic deity, the One God or Allah in Arabic, and although the Tuaregs are theistic, we adopt a slightly different approach. We also believe in Allah, and carry out religious practices in accordance with the Qur'an, but have other indigenous ways. These include belief in spirits, and the soul. The devil, or Iblis, plays a prominent part. Similarly, our distinctive attitude towards death. It must also be stressed that our cultural values emphasise modesty for both sexes. The desert nomads didn't carry out all of the traditional rituals and practices, typically associated with Islam. In particular, fasting during Ramadan, the holy month of the Islamic calendar. Instead they fasted selectively, simply because the practice of

Ramadan fasting conflicted too greatly with a nomadic lifestyle.

I also explained to the Graduate Conference that history has had a substantial impact on what is still happening today to the African Tuaregs. The situation has been exacerbated, and made even more complicated, by the terrorist groups which have grown in number. Their links with corruption within the various governments of the region. So that the *Tenere* has now become a prison for many. Seemingly, without any escape. Moreover a prison that is progressively shrinking in size, due to a number of accelerating developments.

Meanwhile those in the international arena spend millions of dollars on missiles; war planes, and drones. Seeking to control territories from the air which does nothing to sort out the enormous problem below them on the ground. Despite the fact that if only a fraction of this money was used to support positive initiatives in the Sahara, linked initially to education and the media, the results could be a lot different and clearly much more positive.

When the Sahara was under the control of its indigenous native people, the "Tuaregs," there was no evidence of terrorism. Neither was there a massive illegal migration to Europe. Driven at least in part by the machinations of extremists in the countries which they had left. Huge phenomena which continue to trouble the whole world. I believe that whilst the needs of the Tuaregs remain relatively ignored by other countries, these issues will also remain unresolved.

Chapter 3

Hope For An Independent Azawad

I have given an overview in the earlier chapters of what has been happening to the Tuareg people, but let's dig a little deeper now into the history behind the current situation. Including Azawad, the hope and dream which continues to represent our independence and a much better future. Something which many of us continue to believe is still possible. Despite it being a highly complex situation. One which started long before the National Movement For The Liberation Of Azawad or MNLA made a unilateral declaration on 6th April, 2012 that Azawad was to be regarded as an independent state. But then it is often easier when looking back, to see what went wrong. If something doesn't work out the way we think it should, and it is the same here. A number of obstacles and barriers existed at the outset to prevent Azawad's full emergence, and ultimate survival.

Azawad has been easy to find on the map since 1960, when there was the demarcation of the new states. It is effectively a large part of what is now the Republic of Mali, bordering on Mauritania to the west and Niger to the east. As well as Algeria in the north, with Burkina Faso to the south. The total area claimed was eight hundred and twenty two thousand square kilometers. Or sixty six percent of the current area of Mali, equivalent to the whole of France and Belgium combined. The estimated population would have been around four million in 2015. Mostly made up of four ethnic groups of Tuaregs whose common language is Tamacheq. Also, the Arabs who speak Hasania. A dialect that is otherwise spoken mainly in Mauritania, and southern Morocco. Thirdly, a number of the Songhai people. Their language is widely distributed throughout the Sahara, and which is again known as Songhai. Fourth, were the Peul. Their language is a Fulani one from a tribal group which is widespread across west Africa, in particular Niger. The most important towns and cities of the region include the legendary city of Tinbuktu, along with Gao and Kidal.

The very idea of the Tuareg people having a new state was immediately rejected by the other countries in the area. Algeria; Libya; Niger, and Morocco. As if that wasn't enough, it was also rejected by the international community. Led by France; the European Union; Union of African States, and the United Nations. The majority of non-Tuareg ethnicities in the area such as the Fulani; Bambara, and Songhai arranged demonstrations. With acts of violence taking place against the Tuareg people, soon after our independence was declared. The declaration had followed many years of struggle against consecutive governments in Mali where corruption had become rife.

These hostile events took place in Gao; Tinbuktu, and Bamako. Or further afield in Paris, and other European cities. However, the greatest challenge for the Azawad separatists came surprisingly from the Islamist groups in the area. Such as the Ansar Addin; the Movement For Oneness and Jihad in west Africa or MAJO; also Al-Qaida in the Islamic Maghreb or AQIM. All of which have since been criticised for hijacking the independence project, Following an armed and fierce confrontation with members of the MNLA which happened unexpectedly on 27th June, 2012. The conflict ended in the Tuareg revolutionary movement being excluded from the local towns and villages which had partly fallen under the extremists' control.

As a result of the attack the leader of the MNLA, Belal Ag Achareef, was severely injured, He was taken to Burkina Faso by a special helicopter provided by the Burkinabe Government, to receive medical treatment. Before this incident took place the allied Jihadist movements of MAJO; AQIM, and Ansar Dine organised an extensive smear campaign against the MNLA. Targeting the population of Gao and Timbuktu. Although this was mainly against the Songhai and Fulani ethnicities. Abo Alwaled Asaharawi and Mokhtar Bin Belmokhtar, the Algerian leader of Al Qaeda, distributed money and weapons to the Songhai community in Gao. Encouraging them to take to the streets and rally against the MNLA's posts in the city, before Jihadist movements launched a surprise attack on the movement's headquarters. To which the MNLA responded firing live rounds of ammunition into the air above the protestors' heads. Preventing them from ransacking their posts. Twelve people were killed in the attack, together with four detainees, and fourteen others were badly injured. Including Belal Ag Achareef.

Apart from the Jihadist groups' involvement in the situation, why did so many refuse to accept Azawad as an independent state, and this have such an adverse impact on us? The Tuaregs have experienced an increased loss of human rights since then; further suffering; poverty, and hunger. This was undoubtedly due in part to the legacy of French colonialism which still remains, and the region being divided up in Paris during the 1960. But it is also impossible to ignore the subsequent role of the military regimes in Algeria, and other neighbouring countries. Similarly, the internal divisions and tribal conflicts which have challenged Tuareg liberation movements since their second rebellion in 1990. As well as the unfortunate lack of basic organisational competencies, that have existed for many years between the sections of Tuareg society. Last but not least, the hindrance caused by ethnic sub-divisions. Especially among the Songhai; Arabs, and the Fulani people.

As a Tuareg I have seen the damage which a lack of peace has done to so many lives, and I have tried to find the underlying reasons for this. In chapter 9 I compare the

Tuaregs in Niger and other neighbouring countries, to those living in Mali. As a possible means of understanding why they have in the past seemed to be more content with the situation. Whilst the Niger regime successfully hid the idea of a separatist state in the Azawagh and Air Mountains of Northern Niger, from the minds of the Tuareg people there. I will also explain why I believe the Tuareg in Libya and Algeria have not in the past rebelled against their regimes. Despite their political economies not being much better, or the governments much less corrupt, than those in Mali.

The Tuareg ethnicities have been involved in wars since French colonialism came to the Sahara desert during the nineteenth century. Mainly in opposition to the French occupation of our land. Representatives from thirteen European states, the United States of America, and Ottoman Empire held a conference in Berlin during 1885. When they discussed the partition of Africa, and its colonisation. Africans were not invited to the meeting.

A period of colonial activity followed on from this. With the exception of Ethiopia and Liberia, all of the states in Africa today were distributed between the various colonial powers within a few years after the conference. Lines of longitude and latitude, rivers and mountain ranges were used as "artificial borders" separating the colonies. A ruler placed on the map, and a line drawn. It was done without any consideration of African society which was evident at the time, and had been for millennia. Ethnicity and traditional boundaries were simply ignored.

In the years which followed, France expanded its colonial influence from the west African coast to across the Sahel region. Along the southern border of the Sahara into present day Mali, and Niger. Giving it control of the Tuaregs' homeland. The division of Africa was said to have been done pursuant to international law. Ethnic groups, and existing trade routes were severed. My people and others who were affected by this injustice had to accept the problems it caused, and live through what had simply been a paper exercise for those who attended the 1885 conference. Then later, in Paris during 1960. These new borders had little meaning to the Tuaregs. Other than as an ending to their earlier way of life, and traditions. Something which would continue to have an adverse effect on them.

The first engagement with the French colonial army was during 1881 in the Ahaggar Mountains of southern Algeria. Whilst the first rebellion by the Tuaregs against the Malian government, again seeking independence, was in 1963. This was however severely suppressed by the Malian army, supported by France and neighbouring countries. There were many massacres committed against the Tuareg nomads at the time. Hundreds of them were killed, along with their animals. Their wells poisoned, and taxes levied on the use of land for any spurious purpose. Even cutting the dry branches of trees to make a fire became taxable, and this penalty was severely imposed on the Kel Tamachek and the Arab communities.

These unjust measures taken by the Malian regime, supported by France across the years and used against the original inhabitants of the region, caused many Tuaregs to migrate to other neighbouring countries. Algeria; Nigeria, and Mauritania. Whilst some of these migrants ended up as far away as Saudi Arabia. Where there is now in all probability the largest Tuareg community today in exile. Most of these migrations started during 1963 because of the severe crimes which had been committed against the nomads. Followed by a second migration in 1973. This time mainly due to the drought and famine that struck most parts of the Sahel region, leading to a massive loss of animals. Finally, between 1990 and 1994 when there was a second Tuareg rebellion. The largest groups were originally from southern parts of the Azawad region or Arabanda, and places like Tinbuktu. Where tribes such as the Kel Sererry; Imoushagh; Kel Inssar; as well as the black Tuareg, now make up the majority of all the Tuareg people in Saudi Arabia.

On the one hundred and twenty fifth anniversary of the 1885 Berlin conference during 2010, representatives from many African states called for reparation of the wrongs committed by the partition of their continent. They made a statement to the effect that the arbitrary division of Africa amongst the European powers at the time was a crime against humanity. It had ignored African laws; culture; sovereignty, and institutions. They asked for funding to build monuments at historic sites; the return of land, and other resources which had been stolen from them, and the restitution of cultural treasures. Also, formal recognition that colonialism and the crimes committed under it were crimes against humanity. Needless to say, nothing has so far come of this.

Whilst Azawad, or northern Mali as it is known now, continues to experience acute political unrest. Various groups, with different ideologies and political ends, have taken control of the entire region which was declared as Azawad. There is good and bad in every race, and nationality. That is the nature of humanity. This has also played its part in the failure of Azawad becoming a reality. Nevertheless it is still for all of us to make the best life that we can for our families; children; others, and ourselves. Using what we have, to do so. Azawad represents this ideology, and the hope which we have kept alive through the years of conflict in Africa. Quite simply. Our love for the Tenere, the ancient land of the Tuareg nation. Where we firmly believe we can live again in peace.

Although it must also be said that something different needs now to happen, before we can move towards this in a much better way. The change that all of us want to see come about. Without blame being attributed to anyone, or the only thought behind what we do being the pursuance of self interest. Hatred or revenge. These poisonous links to the past in which so many have already died must be untied. An ideal world maybe, but our hope for an independent state of Azawad remains and that is the first step.

This book is a call for peace. It is more than time for it, and the alternative can't be allowed to happen. That the Tuaregs, an ancient race in our world's humanity, survive only in some of the history books and memories of people alive today. The proud and noble blue men who walked the lands of the Sahara desert, with their families and animals.

Our tribal boundaries fragmented, and descendants subjected to endless violence. That something like this which was once inconceivable has been allowed to happen. If for that reason alone it is impossible to forget the Tuaregs, or our Azawad.

Chapter 4

The Legacy of French Neo-Colonialism

"Without Africa, France will slide down into the rank of a third [world] power."
> Jacques Chirac, President of France (1995 - 2007)

"French colonial power has ripped my people, land, and community apart and as scarecrows roaming between newly created colonial borders without taking any consideration for linguistic, color, and culture differences which exist between the Tuareg and black Africans."
> Yusuf Ag Acheikh (Veteran fighter,
> in the 1963 Tuareg uprising)

Let us dig a little deeper again into the history behind all of this. The opposing views quoted above highlight the feelings of many, and the problem which remains today. When France began to occupy our homeland, it was said to be with the intention of controlling the area as a protectorate on our behalf. Within its former colonies throughout the vast region known as French West Africa, and particularly in Bamako. The effect which this has had on present day politics is due to the enormous power of France, and its position as a permanent member of the United Nations Security Council. It also still benefits from historically binding Cooperation Accords which it instigated, with most of its former colonies. The areas which these cover range from security to economic issues. Giving France an ongoing political, and cultural, supremacy over large parts of Africa. All of which is further enhanced by France's role as one of the larger and more proactive states within the European Union.

The first armed friction between the Tuareg people and French colonists occurred in southern Algeria. early in 1881. When Colonel Paul Flatters, who had tried unsuccessfully on two previous occasions to penetrate the Sahara through Ber el Gharama in the far south of Algeria, led a mission into the area. The Colonel and one hundred and ninety eight of his two hundred armed men were killed by a group of Tuareg warriors, led by Amoud Ag Almoukhtar. This was believed to have been done with the help of the harsh Saharan conditions. It sent horror and shock through the heart of the French army who decided to take revenge on behalf of those soldiers who had died.

''The honor of our name, our legitimate influence, the security of our Algerian enterprise, the grandeur and the economy demand that we exact a prompt and energetic revenge for so much bad faith, perfidiousness and ferocity''
(Douglas Porch, The Conquest of the Sahara.)

Nevertheless the French invasion of the Sahara did not go ahead as planned, soon after the massacre of Colonel Flatters' expedition, but not until 1889. Tuareg resistance in the Algerian Sahara continued for many years after this until its leader, Amoud Ag Almoukhtar, escaped to Libya in 1923. He later died there fighting alongside the Libyans in their struggle against the Italians, during 1928. At the same time as the French army was facing fierce resistance in northern Mali. Particularly from the Iwellmedan Kel Atram confederation. This continued until 1927, when the Tuareg soldiers at the time were finally subdued by highly sophisticated French firearms. After thirty four years of sporadic resistance to colonialism in Ahaggar (Algeria); Ajjer (Libya); Aiir and Azawagh (Niger); Adagh and 'the iwellmedan Kel Atram' (Mali). This made the Sahara the last territory in the entire continent to be relinquished for French colonisation.

Even though France has physically left the area in its capacity as a former colonial power, as long as its legacy remains it is not possible to separate the question of Africa in general from the Tuaregs in northern Mali or its adjoining countries. As these are too closely linked. Suffice to say here, having regard to the historical context of what is still occurring, it is notable that France's 2013 military intervention in Mali was only a drop in the ocean. If its prolonged history of intervention for many years throughout the African continent is taken in comparison to this.

As a Tuareg it seems to me that even though France apparently granted independence and autonomy to most of its African colonies, after the 1950s, it didn't relinquish a great deal. Primarily its cultural ties; language; education system; political influence, and most importantly, direct control over the natural resources of the African continent. Especially since this still remains very much the case today. In my opinion, the grant of independence was merely done as an exercise on paper, and a window dressing for continued neo-colonial control.

The binding Cooperation Accords which France asked the colonies to sign described in great detail the nature of their ongoing relationship to each other. Especially regarding economic matters; natural resources; currency; military presence, and security arrangements. France also forced its newly independent states in Africa, including Mali since the 1950s, to pay for the miscellaneous colonial services they had received. These services included the building of factories; roads; airports, and public infrastructure. France also retained the right to seize the national reserves in these countries. Consequently, all those African countries which were previously subject to French colonisation are still obliged to deposit their monetary funds into France's Central Bank. Where eighty percent of the former French colonies' foreign reserves are still controlled by the French treasury. Can this be regarded as true independence?

Fiscal reports indicate that more than five hundred billion USD belonging to African countries are being held in France's treasury. (Hopkins, 1970).

France also retained a first right to purchase any natural resources discovered in its former African colonies. It has reserved the use of this right until no further interest in these resources is specified by it. The African country concerned is entitled then to search for other beneficiaries. Defence clauses were also included in the Cooperation Accords which gave France an absolute right to intervene militarily, and deploy its troops within most of its previous colonies. Particularly when its economic and political interests were considered at risk.

An example of this occurred in northern Mali when France intervened militarily during March, 2013. On the pretext of protecting Malian sovereignty and unity which was allegedly being threatened by the Jihadist movements pushing south. Again with the benefit of hindsight, all was not as it seemed. France had a hidden agenda behind this quick intervention. It was in reality more interested in its former colonies' natural resources: diamonds; uranium, and gold. Mali has been renowned for many centuries for these commodities, and is Africa's third largest gold producer. Perhaps it should not come as a surprise when I say here that French companies have taken control of most of the mines? Similarly, in the north of the region in places like Gao; Samit, and Kidal. Areas which are rich in oil; gold, and uranium.

France has also been intending to extract petroleum at a future date. Especially in the Taoudeni basin, which is at the heart of the land we proposed for Azawad. In addition to its intervention in Mali, France's fundamental goal has been to secure the placement of Areva in neighbouring Niger. Situated less than three hundred kilometers from Kidal. One of the strongholds of the Tuareg rebels, and a further two hundred kilometers from the Tegharghar mountains where the Jihadist groups are usually located.

It is clear that France has also on occasions become increasingly concerned by the intensification of the United States and Chinese activity in Africa. Its subsequent actions confirmed its ongoing interest in the area, and as a possible warning to these major international competitors. Conversely, if Azawad had been successfully established in 2012, the French military would no longer have been able to control the area. Or the use and distribution of these natural resources. Primarily those found in northern Niger, and any which had still to be discovered in the Taoudeni and Tesalit basins.

Considering the colonial agreements binding France and Africa across the years, it is even more apparent why the French decided to intervene as quickly as they did in 2012. Refusing to wait for a decision by the International Security Council which represented its member states. As unlikely as it was, if this had been made in France's favour, this would have allowed it to proceed legally with an intervention. Instead the Jihadist groups who had already moved towards the capital city of Bamako were bombarded by French soldiers, and their special forces made ready to take action.

As you can see from this, the historical ties which continue to connect France to its former colonial states, give it the upper hand and power. To retain control of the lives, and future of the African people. Those who still want to change this ruthless regime, and like the Tuareg people, create a separate state where they can live in peace with their families. It seems likely now that France will not agree to an independent state, such as Azawad, being established in the future. Unless possibly because its military relations and security, with Algeria in particular, have been damaged. Also, to a lesser extent with other neighbouring countries like Mali and Niger, who have witnessed Tuareg rebellions across the years.

History has taught us that Mali has never been able to defeat the rebel factions in the north, without the benefit of external support to defend its borders. Also that when Mali was itself defeated, it went on to turn its guns and weapons on the nomadic Tuareg people and their animals. An old technique used by the Malians, to exert pressure on Tuareg rebels, in an attempt to persuade them to negotiate. Usually somewhere in Algeria which acted as a dominant, self-appointed, mediator since 1990.

My concern remains. What can be done to help my people? The withdrawal of support from France and Algeria would enable the Tuareg insurgencies to succeed in their attempts to gain independence. Neither Mali nor Niger would be able to successfully stand against them, without the help of these major allies. Whilst there are also a number of brave voices, emerging from African nations. Like Mali; Niger; Senegal, and so on.

Those who have the strength, and a compelling force of tradition and culture behind them, to demand something new and better. As in the complete departure of France, and its influence, from the African continent. Whether this is as a military power; economically, or otherwise. Giving the Tuareg people at long last the fulfilment of their wishes, and hope. Together with the return of their human rights, and capacity to handle their own future and affairs.

I firmly believe that the Tuareg call for Azawad, our own independent state, is still there... It should no longer remain unheard.

Photographs

Akli Sh'kka speaking to the United Nations in 2016.

Akli Sh'kka speaking to an audience to the United Nations Indigenous
Forum in 2016

Tuareg fighters in the 1990's rebellion.

Other Tuareg fighters in the 1990's rebellion, with a Malian soldier whom they had taken prisoner.

31

Malian soldiers following Zeid Ag Attaher, Leader of 1963 rebellion (Middle). He had been captured by the Algerians and extradited to Mali Along with Ilyas Ag Ayouba (right) and Mahmmed Alhassan Ag Intwdou (left). All of whom had been made to remove their turbans, which is an insult to a Tuareg man.

Tuareg soldiers in the Libyan army, before they were sent to Lebanon and Chad by Colonel Qadafi during the early 1980s.

Akli Sh'kka in the Sahara with a group of Tuareg children. This photograph was taken in 2008. Whilst he was making the documentary film, Imshuradj, or People Without A Country.

More Tuareg Fighters In Libya.

Iyad Aghali, leader of the 1990 Tuareg rebellion (middle), with Ayss Ag Ouerakoul alongside kneeling on his arm.

Iyad Ag Aghali in Algeria, signing the 1991 peace agreement with Mali.

The MNLA's leaders on the 1st November, 2010 when it was established. Mohammed Jeri Maiga; Belal Ag Acharif, and Mahmoud Ali (from left to right).

Chapter 5

Conflicting Divisions in The Tuareg Liberation Movements

"It is very puzzling that internal divisions among the Tuareg only open up at times of collective rebellion, after they have taken up arms against a common enemy. Once the unity of Mali is reinstated however, they seem to get on alright again."

Mashaknani (a Tuareg leader)

When looking at the reasons why Azawad didn't succeed in 2012, we need to explore the historical divisions that existed between the people who were supporting it. The conflict between the various Tuareg factions involved in the MNLA, and Le Groupe Autodéfense Touareg Imghad et Alliés or GATIA. A pro-government Tuareg and Arab Group in northern Mali, established by General Alhaji Ag Gamo. Despite the fact that he was a Tuareg, he refused to recognise the concept of an independent Azawad state. Choosing instead to lead the Imghad tribe, along with their Arab and Bambara allies, during the 2012 conflict. In place of the Malian army, after it had been severely defeated on a number of occasions. Also continuing its attempts to ensure that Azawad did not survive. As you can well imagine, this contributed to the lack of good organisation within the MNLA itself, and ultimately, the failure of Azawad.

Nevertheless, in my opinion, the 2012 Tuareg rebellion against the Malian government was one of the most successful since the first uprising in 1963, and the 1990s. Irrespective of the problems within the MNLA at that time, which not only included inter-tribal conflict and disunity amongst the leaders, but also a failure to attract other ethnic groups into its ranks. Such as the Fulani; Songhoi; Arabs; and other Tuareg tribes, like the Imghad.

Looking back now several years later, it is easy to see that disunity and internal tribal wars between different Tuareg groups was always going to be a huge obstacle to the realisation of Azawad. Or any independence elsewhere in the region. The varying lifestyles of those involved in the situation had been an integral part of the problem for too many years. As a result, the Tuareg nation now remains divided between five states: Libya; Algeria; Niger; Burkina Faso, and Mali. An area covering five million square kilometers.

Sadly it is not possible in this book for me to tell you about every single episode which has been a part of the much broader picture, and history leading to the 2012 Tuareg uprising. Although many of these events contributed to what happened then. Much of it also occurred simultaneously. For that reason alone, I have used subtitles when talking about some of the splinter groups which formed mostly between the 1990s and 2012. So that it is easier to follow their progress, and differentiate them. The main group largely involved in the inception of Azawad remains the MNLA, and which I believe ought to have been completely successful.

Popular Front For The Liberation Of Azawad

During the earlier rebellions in 1990 and 1994, Tuareg leaders found themselves roughly split into four separate fronts. Each of which corresponded to a single Tuareg tribe, or region. The effect of this fragmentation was that the main collective body at the time, the Popular Front for the Liberation of Azawad, also quickly divided into five or six separate armed tribal groups. Sometimes these groups would turn their guns on each other. Or become allied to other ethnic groups, which again happened for political reasons.

When the Popular Movement of Azawad was created in January, 1991 it consisted mainly of the Ifoghas tribe. Led by Iyad Ag Aghali, and Acheikh Ag Awassa. Iyad was a national patriot at the outset. Fighting for the freedom; rights, and needs of his own people. But in the 2012 revolution he changed, and turned into a hardline Jihadist. Fighting unmercilessly for the unity of the state of Mali under Sharia law. Ag Aghali and his religious group, Ansar Adin which later became Jama'at Nasr al-Islam wal Muslimin. also rejected the idea of an independent state for the Tuareg people in northern Mali. Preferring to pursue the idea of an Islamic state which would cover the whole country.

Despite the internal tribal and ethnic divisions among the Tuareg separatists also being present at different levels in the earlier rebellions of 1963 and the 1990s, there was however a significant difference in 2012. Essentially the new and violent internal conflicts which arose were based on different goals, and new socio-political agendas.

Azawad Arab Islamic Front

The members of this movement mostly came from the Arab community in Mali. In particular Gao; Taoudeni, and Tinbuktu. The group was led by Ahmed Ould Sidi Mohammed, an Arab businessman and cigarette smuggler from Tinwkar, a small village in north east Gao. It was set up in January, 1991 to defend the Arab population, allegedly from Tuareg attacks. It was however responsible for many war crimes against people from the Tuareg tribes. A number of activists in the movement repeatedly accused the Tuareg separatists of trying to establish a state which would be entirely centered on their own ethnic group. That Azawad would inevitably disregard other races, like the

Arabs and Songhai. It would also be responsible for causing other Berbers in North Africa, to rise up against their respective governments.

These arguments resonated well with pan-Arab nationalists, and other politicians in north Africa. Who believed that the creation of an Azawad state in northern Mali might well encourage other Tuaregs from southern Algeria; Libya, and Niger to rise up in a similar fashion. The borders of such a state might eventually extend far beyond Mali. Even perhaps as far as those parts of north Africa where the majority of the population were Amazigh Berbers. Another branch of the wider Tuareg nation. This could also provoke others into demanding a separate state of their own. This concern was partially reflected in the increasing calls made for one Amazigh national state across north Africa. There have been a variety of campaigns across the years for a new state which would include all of the Berber people in north Africa.

One proposed state called Tamazgha would have stretched across the Sahara from the Siwa Oasis in western Egypt, to the Canary Islands further west. There was also talk of it running west across northern Libya. So that it would embrace Tunisia; Algeria; Morocco, and Mauritania. Then south into southern Mali, and Niger. This was far beyond the original plan for Azawad the 2012 separatists had in mind, and would have included western Spain.

Some of the more fanatical Amazigh activists were heard to call for the repatriation of descendants of those Arabs who travelled west during the eighth century. To send them back to the place where their ancestors originated, with the Islamic message they were propagating! More specifically, the Arabian Peninsula, or Aljazeera Al Arabiya in Arabic.

The Revolutionary Liberation Army of Azawad

This group was created in November, 1991 when the Imghad tribe was at war with the Ifoghas Tuareg people. This bitter conflict resulted in the violent death of dozens of people on both sides. Not only armed fighters but also unarmed, innocent, Tuaregs. The same thing happened again, twenty years later in 2012, with even more bloodshed and loss of life. On this occasion the founder and leader of the later group GATIA, Colonel Alhaji Ag Gamou, declared a full blown war against the MNLA before setting up a tribal group. He had been in charge of the official Malian army in Gao; Menka; Tassalit, and Kidal. So was well known for wielding his authority with an iron hand. The majority of the army he still commanded were his own tribesmen, the Imghad. At the time, most black Malians in the south regarded him as a national hero. His efforts had led to the unity of their region, and ultimately, Azawad being destroyed. On 31st March, 2012 Alhaji and his six hundred hundred men, including high ranking officers from the Malian army, were expelled from north Mali by MNLA fighters. They sought refuge in neighbouring Niger.

He returned in July, 2012 freshly armed, and with strong support from Niger. By August, 2014 his mission for GATIA was to chase the MNLA separatists out of the region, along with their allies. Making it very clear that GATIA was fighting to retain the integrity of the existing state of Mali, and ensure Azawad would not survive. Of course, this meant that Alhaji Ag Gamou had changed sides. During the 1990s he was one of the most prominent leaders and military commanders who fought fiercely against the Malian state in an attempt to ensure the success of Azawad. Whereas a few years later, he was completely rejecting any possibility of this happening. Calling its supporters bandits; terrorists, and criminals that must be put on trial!

As a result the former Azawad Revolutionary Liberation Army was back, but under a new name, GATIA. Its members were mostly the Tuareg Imghad people, and their allies. It is likely that this group's main objective also involved settling old scores with their traditional enemy, the Ifoghas tribe. The leaders thought they would be able to destroy them once and for all, under the convenient banner of fighting for the national unity of Mali. Many human rights crimes were committed by both sides in the conflict which ensued. The GATIA militia exploited their connection to the legitimate Malian army. With strong support from the black citizens in the area who were also opposed to Azawad.

The Popular Front of Azawad (MPA)

The Popular Front of Azawad or MPA was created in January, 1991. Its members were mostly from the Ifoghas tribe. The founders of the movement, including Iyad Ag Aghali and Acheikh Ag Awssa, were committed to fighting the Malian army; protecting civilians from Malian armed militia like the Songhai, and also defending the Ifoghas tribe from other movements. Split up during the Tamnghasst Pact which had been signed in Algeria during 1991. It's likely that the MPA was created by the Ifoghas and their allies, to stand against the Imghad tribes. Hundreds of innocent Tuaregs were killed on both sides. As a result of hit and run attacks which continued for almost a year. The conflict subsequently spilled over into Libya and Algeria where many Tuaregs lived and worked.

Azawad National Liberation front

The ANLF was created in January, 1993. The group's members were mostly from the Ishadanharene and Douss'hak tribes in the Menka region. Regarded as the harbingers of the 2012 rebellion. The Douss'hak people joined GATIA during May, 2016. Moussa Ag

Acharatoumane who also helped establish the MNLA, had become closer to the Bamako than Azawad cause.

By 2016 the majority of the Douss'hak tribe had broken away from the MNLA, and created their own movement, the MSA. Whilst the Ishadanharen tribe remained loyal to the MNLA. The latter had gained considerable success in many areas as a political and armed group, in comparison to previous Tuareg rebellions, but still couldn't make an inroad into all of the Tuareg people. Let alone the other Malian ethnic groups.

It is easy to appreciate the movement's lack of unity from this, and the contribution which it must have made to the failure of Azawad during 2012. Culminating in the MOJWA terrorist group attacking the MNLA's Headquarters in Gao. With its leader, Belal Ag Ashareef and the MNLA's General Secretary, being almost killed in the conflict.

Belal was criticised for not having had full control of his military commanders and soldiers. Nevertheless, despite his orders not always being followed, he is still regarded now by many young Tuareg men and women as a moderate leader. One who was trying to do his best to create a unified military and political movement which didn't rely on tribal affiliations.

The lack of unity in the MNLA had in fact been apparent since its inception in the Zakak Mountains during November, 2011. Iyad Ag Aghali wasn't given the leadership of the group by members of the MNLA at that time, so set up his own religious movement, the Ansar Addin. Even right at the beginning, many of the soldiers and Ifoghas' traditional leaders of the MNLA deserted not long afterwards, to join the Ansar Addin. The most notable of which was Alghabass Ag Intalla, one of the most senior

Ifoghas leaders and son of Amanokal N Adagh, Intala Ag Attaher.

Despite the criticisms of Belal's leadership, the smooth running of the MNLA was also surprisingly even more complicated than this. Each tribe within the movement was led by its own traditional leader. As a result, its soldiers did not take direct orders from Belal. Only from their own tribal leaders also within the movement. The Idnan tribe were a good example of this. They were led by the MNLA's military chief of staff, Mohammed Ag Najim. Yet neither he nor his tribesmen completely followed orders issued by Belal.

This scenario can be applied to other leaders within the movement, for example, the Shaman-amass tribe. In 2012, this was led militarily by Colonel Assalatte Ag Khaby. He defected from the MNLA soon after the independence declaration, and joined Ansar Addin. Subsequently accused by the members of the MNLA of being "two-faced," and changing his loyalty whenever he chose! Perhaps that isn't so far from the truth? According to many of the MNLA leaders and activists who were at one time close to him, he didn't seem sufficiently passionate about the idea of Azawad, or convinced that it could exist. It seems likely that he joined the MNLA movement in its early days, to protect himself and his tribe from other hardline groups in the area. Such as the Ansar Adin, and AQIM.

Whilst tribes like the Taghtmellt; Kel Assouk; Ishadanharen; Eradjnaten, and Ifoghas were also organised under Belal Ag Ashareef's authority as an Ifoghas political leader, they were again only loyal to their traditional leaders. They did not take orders from Belal, or his Chief of Staff, Mohammed Najim.

The other problem may have been that the MNLA was dominated by the Ifoghas, and their affiliated Tuareg tribes

43

who were mostly from the Kidal region. The main leaders like Belal were from the Ifoghas tribe. This gave Malian government supporters the opportunity to criticise the movement for failing to represent the Tuareg community as a whole or the entire region.

Nevertheless, irrespective of the criticisms levelled against the MNLA, it was able to gain more legitimacy amongst the Tuareg people than any other movement in recent history. It created a massive change in what had been happening for many years. Particularly amongst the young; the women; and above all, educated and political classes. This can also be attributed to the power of social media; Facebook, and WhatsApp. Similarly, television, and radio outlets. All of which played an important role in attracting different people to the liberation movement's ranks.

A new generation of educated young Tuaregs strongly supported the 2012 revolution at home, and abroad. It was the first time in the history of our insurgencies that the media had been used in favour of a cause that had been ongoing for many years. It can also be said that this was the first time the Tuareg people revolted, with the support of the public. Things had changed for the better! Ours was no longer a single leader revolution, but had become a people revolution.

The MNLA may not have been entirely successful in its attempt during 2012 but, I believe it did a great deal to contribute to the future of an independent Tuareg state.

Chapter 6

Resistance From Ethnic Groups In Mali

Ethnic differences also exist among the people of Mali and which again helped contribute to the failure of Azawad. The Songhai and Bambara ethnicities both have different cultures to the Tuaregs. Guerrilla conflicts occurred between these opposing groups, and crimes against human rights were committed by both sides in 2012 and earlier.

The Tuareg people strongly believed in their declaration that Azawad should become an independent state. To us it represented a fair and reasonable demand for a small amount of justice, after two centuries of outrageous maltreatment. Mostly by the French government. This had been followed by an unfriendly domination of new élites in those states which succeeded France's régime in west Africa. The leaders of these countries often had little or no sympathy for those whom they regarded as "uppity nomads," and were amongst other things difficult to tax!

Quite often the Tuareg people form a small minority in comparison to the other tribes, or people such as the Songhai. Soon after the declaration of independence in 2012, hundreds of Songhai in Bamako and Gao took to the streets to denounce it. Many demonstrators spoke to the media. Claiming that the Azawad area did not belong to the Tuaregs, but was instead Songhai and Peul territory. While the triangular area we wished to claim for Azawad in northern Mali had been our traditional homeland for centuries.

These ethnic differences became such a problem that by 2018 there was another bloody war in full swing, between the different factions and militias with an alleged interest in northern Mali. I would like to say here that it is again not my intention to take sides in any way. Or to pass judgment on the behaviour of the individuals who were involved, whether directly or indirectly, in events at that time. I wrote this book as a call for peace. To ask that all of us now look beyond what has happened. So that we can instead work towards creating a much better future for everyone, without violence and suffering.

The history of this part of the modern state of Mali, and of earlier Tuareg rebellions in the area, goes a long way to reminding us that ethnic divisions and mutual enmity have been around for a long time. Although in essence most of the conflicts are between the lighter skinned Tuareg nomads, and sedentary black Malians. In the past the diverse people of this vast area lived together in relative harmony for countless decades, with remarkably few problems. But whenever the Tuareg nomads chose to make an armed challenge against the government of Mali in Bamako, any such harmony quickly dissolved. The other tribal people to the south from related ethnic groups subsequently united against the Tuaregs, who were regarded throughout as coming from much farther north. Ever since Mali obtained its independence in 1960, these ethnic conflicts have taken place approximately every ten years in the north.

During the 1990's, many black Songhai and Peul joined forces to create armed militias, to prevent Tuareg rebels from pushing southwards. One of the most prominent of these groups established at that time was the Ganda Koy militia, which originated as a Songhai initiative in opposition to the Tuareg rebellion, and was intended to block any hope of independence. The movement was set up in May, 1994 by a former officer from the Malian armed forces, Imam Mohammed n'Tissa Maiga. The official name of the group was the Patriotic Malian Movement Ganda

Koy or MPGK. Ganda Koy can be translated from the Songhai language as masters of the land, or landowner.

Most of those who joined the Ganda Koy, including the leaders, were defectors from the Malian army. Earlier generations of the Tuaregs, seen as a warrior people, regarded both of those tribes as their vassals or slaves. This was particularly so in the case of the Peul minority. The history of servitude between these tribes partly explains why, ever since the Tuareg rebellion of the 1990's, the Songhai and Peul fighters have aligned themselves with the Malian government. To put down Tuareg uprisings in the north. Perhaps also with a view of liberating themselves from these historical shackles?

It is said that the main reason why both the Peul and Songhai are against the idea of an independent Azawad state is because they are still worried the Tuareg people from the north might try again to subjugate them. When that is far from the case, but this illustrates just how deeply these ethnic conflicts can run. Both the Songhai and Peul also see themselves as a native people, indigenous to their own lands. Whilst perceiving the Tuaregs as invaders who came from north Africa many years ago to plunder. For that reason we are regarded as not having the right to make decisions on anyone else's behalf. Particularly in relation to the future of what the black community of the Songhai and Peul identify, as their legitimate and historic homeland.

During the 1990 and 1991 Tuareg rebellions, the Malian army gave extensive arms and cash to the Ganda Koy militia. On the understanding that they would attack any light skinned Tuaregs or Arabs that they could find. The Ganda Koy are also said to have targeted anyone who might possibly have had sympathy for the rebels. As well as those suspected of giving support to the idea of an independent Azawad. Hundreds of Tuareg civilians were killed. Their houses destroyed, and their animals, either killed or taken from the owners. Possibly the most blatant crime to be found in the collective memory of Tuareg nomads was that committed by the Ganda Koy militia during October, 1994 with the full support of the Malian Army. Fifty three Tuareg marabouts or holy men mostly from the Kel Assouk tribe, along with women (including those who were pregnant) and children, were massacred at a camp near Gao. This horrific atrocity still lingers in the minds of the Tuareg people throughout the Sahara.

Whenever there is a rebellion in the north, the Malian government unleashes its army with the intention of killing the vulnerable Tuareg nomads. The main aim of this is to send fear into the hearts of the rebels. Persuading them to surrender their arms, then sit around a table for unequal and unproductive negotiations. As part of these submissive tactics by the Malian army, more than one hundred and fifty thousand Tuareg nomads fled during 2012. Going to Burkina Faso; Algeria, or Mauritania. The majority of these refugees were either Tuareg nomads or El-Bidan. In Arabic, El-Bidan means "whites." This is mainly used by the Tuaregs to describe the Arabs in Mali; Niger; the Moroccan Sahara, and Mauritania.

Even from these few examples it is easy to see the adverse effect which this mutual hatred, between the Tuareg minority and a majority of black Malians (Songhai and Peul), has had on the establishment and survival of Azawad. Arguments involving ethnic or racial prejudice have been used by both sides when seeking allies or sympathy. As well as to gain legitimacy for their own political ends.

The Ganda Koy movement emphasized the idea of the existence of a war between 'blacks' and 'whites' in order to attract 'bellah' (Peul) and 'el-Haratin' to their side, the latter Arabic term refers to semi-servile peoples. (Judith Scheele, 2012)

Sadly this scenario has been repeated, again and again. On April 6th, 2012 hundreds of protesting Songhai and Peul took to the streets of Gao which had by then been proclaimed the capital of Azawad. Also in Bamako, the capital of Mali, to show their rejection of it. There were even demonstrations as far away as in Europe. Among those most active in circulating hatred on social media (Facebook in particular), and during demonstrations and campaigns of violence, were a number of Songhai in the north. Together with other Malian blacks, further south in Bamako. The hostile slogans they used included: "Azawad NO! YES, for the unity of Mali. And "northern Mali DOES NOT belong to the white Tuareg people!"

On the day before the declaration of Azawad, hundreds of Songhai and black Africans supported by the MAJUA group and AQIM, took to the streets of Gao in massive demonstrations. Announcing their refusal to Mali being split into two countries, with an independent Azawad in the north. The Ganda Koy militia quickly reformed, and reorganised itself, to begin targeting Tuareg civilians and MNLA members. Just as they had done in previous years. In a statement released in January 2012, the Ganda Koy militia formally declared their opposition to Azawad, and that it would not allow Mali to be divided.

This statement also demanded that all Malians should unite, and defend their native country from the invaders and bandits. It was soon followed by a move to target Tuareg and Arab "whites" in the Malian capital, Bamako. All whites became legitimate targets. Their houses; shops, and other property were torched. As a result of these appalling events many of the victimised population fled the capital to the neighbouring countries of Mauritania and Burkina Faso. The Ganda Koy also attacked the camps of the Tuareg nomads near Gao in the same way.

Media messages sent out repeatedly by the Ganda Koy publicised their absolute refusal to allow a Tuareg independent state, or even permit a separate state-within-a-state in the northern part of the country. Whilst the MNLA presented themselves vigorously as a revolutionary new movement, that was intended to liberate ALL the people of Azawad. Whether they were Tuareg; Arab; Peul, or Songhai.

When the MNLA was initially formed in 2010, it developed from a peaceful political group which mainly consisted of Tuaregs, Songhai and Arabs. Known in French as, Le Movement National de Libération de l'Azawad. It went on to become a military-political movement in 2012, that began to rely on weapons and strong dialogue to pursue its goals. In an open letter dated 1st November, 2010 the same day as the movement was set up in Gao, the leaders said that they had been forced to change their plans. They could no longer be a peaceful movement but an armed political one, because the Malian Government had refused their offer to negotiate.

There is evidence of violence towards other tribal and ethnic factions from the very beginning, and it is clear that the MNLA leaders did fail to attract other ethnic groups to their idea of an independent state. One that was intended to be for the benefit of the diverse, and widely scattered, population in this area. Namely, the Songhai and Fulani. Given the long history of conflict between these ethnicities, I am not surprised that it failed in this regard. Both groups had a majority in places like Gao, and Tinbuktu.

This city was established by the Tuareg people in the fifteenth century. Its name originated from a legendary Tuareg woman called Buktu. Camel caravans carrying salt came there from the Taoudani region; Morocco, and Mauritania. They left their goods with Buktu for safe keeping. As time passed, the town became a regular stopping place along the trading routes. Whether those who arrived there came from further south; west; or east, the salt traders began to call it Tinbuktu. Meaning the place of Buktu... in the Tuareg language.

Chapter 7

The Role of Neighbouring States In The Failure Of Azawad

The first Islamist movement which arrived in southern Mali during the 1990s was the Tablighi Jamaat group. Its origins were in Pakistan. The members preached its dawa, an Arabic word meaning a call. Indicating that it was a peaceful, Islamic group. Trying to distance itself from politics and violence. Nevertheless many people regard it as the beginning of extremism, and radical Islam in the region. Although there had been other Islamist militants in Algeria for many years. Like the Salafist Group for Preaching and Combat which was founded by the Algerian extremist, Hassan Hattab, during the civil war of 1998. But none of these militant groups had made their way into northern Mali until 2003. Before the Salafist Group for Preaching and Combat began to operate under the name of AQIM during 2007, it was a local Algerian Islamist movement whose aim was to change the existing Algerian military regime into an Islamic state.

The situation escalated in April, 2003, when thirty-two European tourists were kidnapped in the Ahaggar mountains of southern Algeria. Three weeks after their disappearance, reports began to suggest that the hostages had ended up in the Tigharghar mountains of northern Mali. They were eventually released after three months of negotiations with the Malian officials. These were led by Iyad Ag Aghali who would later in 2012 become a leader for the extremist Ansar Addin group. As part of this process, five million euros were paid in cash to the abductors through Ag Aghali.

After this the Americans and Europeans began to take more of an interest in what was happening in northern Mali. Given that it had gradually become a potential safe haven for different illegal groups. Terrorists; drug dealers; cigarette smugglers; human, and arms traffickers. Whilst Kidal was a well-known stronghold for Tuareg rebels, opposing the Malian government, after the country became independent from France in 1960.

The 2012 events in northern Mali led to the total collapse of the elected authorities. A military coup d'état on March 21st from a junta, led by Captain Amadou Sanogo, was followed by the Azawad declaration on April 6th. A period of less than three months in which hit and run guerrilla warfare took place between Tuareg rebels and the Malian Army. These unforeseen events precipitated another cycle of violence throughout the entire region. People who lived through this were shocked by the rapid changes. In particular, the unexpected rise of the well-equipped radical Islamist movements in the area who quickly seized control of large parts of the region. After pushing out the MNLA from its last stronghold in the city of Gao on June 26th, 2012. These radical groups included the Ansar al-Dine or Defenders of the Faith; AQIM; and the Movement for Oneness and Jihad in West Africa or MUJAO.

The leader of Ansar al-Dine, Iyad Ag Aghali, released an official statement written in Arabic. This was subsequently reiterated by the group's military spokesman, Oumara Ham: It declared that their war was for Islam, and the application of Sharia law throughout Mali. Not only did they reject Azawad, but would not allow it to become established. The Ansar Addin were against all secular movements who wanted a separate state in northern Mali.

The same hostile rhetoric towards the Tuaregs was used by the leader of AQIM, Abdelmalek Droukdel. Also sometimes known as, Abu Musab Abdel Wadoud. He said during a video statement released in June, 2012 that this group wanted a united Mali under Islamic Sharia law. He went on to say that France had been lying to the people of Mali when it indicated that it didn't want a divided country. The reality was it had been supporting the Azawad Liberation Movement. It was a matter now of thanking God that their Mujahedeen brothers and Muslim sons in the north had destroyed this Satanist project and saved Mali from partition!

Strong political rhetoric that led to these three Islamist movements joining together to end the military role of the MNLA, and stand against our dream of an independent state. There were some unverified reports about alliances being made between Jihadist groups and the MNLA, particularly the Tuareg Islamist national group Ansar Addin, but these proved to be either non-existent or very weak links. What is certain is that the MNLA's leaders spent a long time trying to convince the Ansar Addin to distance itself from transnational radical movements. Such as Al-Qaeda, and instead, to join forces with the MNLA. These attempts obviously had the opposite effect, and led eventually to the establishment of pro-Malian and western media. Both of which played a part in spreading confusion within the MNLA.

The reaction of governments in those countries which border Mali also had a detrimental effect. Namely Algeria; Libya, and Niger. This was primarily linked to geopolitics; the control of natural resources in the area; and a scattered Tuareg population.

During the 1963 Tuareg uprising, Algeria supported the Malian government politically and militarily, to quash the Alfellaga rebellion. The principal leaders were arrested and extradited to Mali when they sought refuge in Algeria. This was done as a "gift" for Modibo Kita, the first Malian President. Their names were Zeyd Ag Attaher, and Alladi

Ag Albasher. Of the thirty five others who suffered the same fate, these included Mahmmed Mahmoud; El Araouani, Mohammed Ali; Taher Ansari; Ilyas Ag Ayouba, and Sidalmin Ag Acheikh.

When the 1970s drought struck most parts of the Sahara desert, and many Tuareg nomads lost their animals and livestock, they were forced to live inside overcrowded settlements. Several of these were located on the edge of developing towns in southern Algeria, and Libya. Then quite unexpectedly in 1980, Colonel Qaddafi invited the Tuareg people to join him in Libya. He admitted that it was their original homeland in the Sahara. He also made a number of promises to the Tuaregs of what they would receive if they came to his country. These included good housing; free education; and help with military training. To enable them to liberate their traditional lands in both Azawad or Mali, and Air-Azawagh in Niger. He even promised Libyan nationality to those who wanted it. His call went as far as Tinbuktu. Hundreds of young Tuaregs from all over the Sahara soon made their way to Libya, in response to his invitation and call to arms. Determined to build a better life for themselves by seizing this opportunity.

When they arrived in Libya Qaddafi's officials installed them in marginal locations. Telling them that these would only be temporary. They were very much like refugee camps, but the Tuaregs were led to believe that they would soon be given much better living accomodation in the light of Colonel Qaddafi's well-publicised promises. Before very long however, it became quite clear that his famous speech was simply political rhetoric. He had no intention whatsoever of providing genuine support for the Tuareg people. Never mind helping them successfully achieve their dream of becoming independent. After some elementary military instruction many of the so-called Ishumar, or men who had made their way to Libya at that time, realised that they had been completely deceived. Despite their unwillingness, many were constrained into fighting for him. Helping Qaddafi pursue his own personal wars in Lebanon and Syria during 1982, and Chad in 1978.

It is quite clear now that his main purpose all along had been to recruit more soldiers for his own, weakened, army. When he went to Lebanon, as a Great Arab Liberator, it was to oppose Israel in what came to be known as the Lebanon War. He already knew how capable and fierce the Tuareg fighters were and he exploited them, seemingly without any qualms whatsoever. Many Tuareg men who had answered his call to come to oil-rich Libya, left their families behind in the Sahara. No one in the stateless-refugee ghettos had identification, or citizen's rights. Never mind a nationality, or a passport. Against the older people's wishes, the Tuareg young had been sent to fight in hopeless wars that Qaddafi eventually lost. In Chad, as well as Lebanon. Many of those Tuaregs, if not killed or badly injured, simply disappeared.

An unnecessary tragedy, and yet all was not lost. Although Qaddafi unmercilessly used the Tuareg people for his own purposes, he indirectly offered helpful support from which some did benefit. Not only did they take advantage of the military training that he provided, but more importantly, his education system. Hundreds gained access to schooling which enabled them later to go to university, and which is already having an effect on the possible future of Azawad. Even more unexpectedly, a few Tuaregs became high ranking officers in the Libyan army. In 1990, some of these soldiers managed to return to Mali to start a new rebellion. They included Iyad Ag Aghali, Sidikham Ag Mohammed; Issa Gova; Asslat Ag Khabi; Abdurhmane Galla, and Alhaji Ag Gamou.

All this is not to say that I have forgotten the Tuaregs who died at this time, suffered horrific injuries, or simply disappeared. Which happened to so many of my people. Including those who were arrested by the Qaddafi military, and imprisoned for three years on charges of attempting to smuggle weapons into Mali or Niger. Including Khamlamin Alla; Mahmmed Didi (aka Jackson); Iyad Mossa; and Mohammed Najem, who became Chief of Staff for the MNLA's army during 2012. These men were caught whilst trying to smuggle an AK-47, and ammunition, out of Libya.

Looking at the conflict which has also existed between Algeria and the Tuareg people across the years, its government helped quash the 1963 rebellion led by Alla Ag Albacher and others. Among them was Zeida Ag Attaher who later sought refuge and protection from the Algerian authorities, but this didn't go according to plan. Instead of finding a place of safety, along with many other Tuaregs, he was extradited to Bamako and imprisoned for 15 years.

According to former members of the 1990 uprising, Algeria also infiltrated the ranks of that rebellion by attempting to assassinate its leaders. Iyad Ag Aghali, and Abrurhmane Galla. The first attempt to eliminate Iyad made by the Algerian secret service took place during August, 1990 in Achabrech. A valley near the Algerian border with Mali. Men from the Algerian Department of Intelligence and Security or DRS stopped a four by four Toyota which they believed belonged to Iyad. His driver, Aghali, was however alone in the vehicle while out looking for gazelle.

The Algerians have created as much pressure as possible for the members of every Tuareg rebellion. This caused enormous difficulties in the 1990s, when the Algerian army and police began to arrest all Tuareg males in Tinzaparin; Timyawen; Tamanghasset, and elsewhere. Irrespective of their age, and on suspicion of them supporting the rebels. One hundred men and women were detained for carrying symbols of the revolution. The Algerians even went as far as including the Tinariwen Band's music cassettes in this exercise. Anyone who might be suspected of supporting the cause was imprisoned without trial. More often than not without any conclusive evidence to establish their "guilt!"

The purpose of these hostilities was again intended to put more pressure on the rebels. Whose strongholds were located at Kidal; Menka, and in the Tigharghar mountains. The Algerians hoped that they would surrender their arms, and which would again give them an opportunity of bringing the separatists together around one table with the Malian government. Following the established pattern, these negotiations would be supervised by the Algerian authorities.

Even now Algeria considers itself as the only rightful mediator, with full authority to review and control the Tuaregs' case. Whether this is within, or outside their region. This situation occurs every time there is a new revolt in the north. Since the rebellion in 1990's, this has given Algeria the opportunity to manipulate negotiations between the Tuaregs and the Malian government. Often involving the creation of adverse agreements, to ensure that every step of the process remains under their control. Obviously not allowing autonomy, or an independent state like Azawad.

In 2012 many Tuareg activists and leaders also criticised Algeria for injecting terrorist groups into the north. In an attempt to confuse the legitimate rebellion, and once again destroy our prospect of independence. This came to light when former members of the Ansar Addin Group spoke about their secret engagements with the DRS during May, 2013.

I believe that the Algerian government sought to exert this control out of self-interest, and also possibly fear. Given that Azawad would have bordered on Algerian land in the south. Where it had a large Tuareg population with the potential to rise up, and add more weight to the political demand for Azawad. Even possibly seeking to join us in our new state.

Whilst in Niger, where many Tuareg rebellions took place between the 1990s and 2007, the government also took an aggressive stand against Azawad. It is possible that Niger even went so far as supporting the Malian army, and its pro-government group GATIA, by sending some of its own soldiers to fight alongside them. Self-interest and corruption again played a part in this, with the desire to control the existence of natural resources in the area which had been declared as Azawad. Oil; gas, and uranium in those places where the Tuareg people had traditionally lived. All of which obviously continue to have a considerable monetary value.

My people had previously been digging for gold on a large scale in Kidal; the Tessalit Basin; Zakak, and Ahzraghen. Areas which are now in northern Mali; Niger, and Southern Algeria. Reliable local reports at the time estimated the total amount of gold extracted was approximately two tons per month. There have also been many reports from the inhabitants of northern Mali that members of the French Army, as well as some of the United Nations' forces, were secretly involved in digging for their own gold. Most of this activity was in or around Kidal, and the Tessalit basin. In 2013, Algeria closed its border with northern Mali. Touching on the area we had designated for Azawad. The Algerian government said that they had done this to protect their national wealth from illegal trespassers. This led to hundreds of young Tuaregs being arrested and imprisoned without trial on charges of illegal gold mining inside Algeria.

Chapter 8

The 2020 Coup D'Etat And Democratic Sham In Mali

All of this led to another coup taking place in 2020. The reasoning behind it was that Mali had become a failed state. Throughout its long history, every government has come to power following a military coup. So that this is now the political norm. It will remain the case unless the Tuareg people in the north regain their independence, and Mali becomes a properly run, democratic country. Not as it currently stands. Or at the very least Azawad people have some sort of federalism, and autonomy, to handle their own affairs. Instead of this, terrorism has been increasing, and the main issue behind the 2020 coup was the deep seated corruption within the Malian government. Coupled with a lack of fair distribution of resources, and power. Governments in the region, including Mali, have been using terrorists to secure funding from the West; United Nations, and European Union. Complicating even further Tuareg historical, and legitimate cause for independence.

Democracy is defined as a system of government by the whole population of an area through its elected representatives. This has clearly not been happening in Mali, and to such an extent that the process has become a complete sham. Resulting in the streets of Bamako being filled with jubilant crowds on 18th August, 2020 celebrating the latest coup d'état which had taken place. It had followed a series of protests against irregularities in the re-election of President Ibrahim Boubacar Keita. Again, mostly concerning allegations of corruption, and fraud. It wasn't long before the President and his prime minister, Boubou Cisse, were arrested. Then taken to the Kati military base where the mutiny had started. The President resigned later during a television interview which seemed to confirm that he didn't have any choice in the matter.

Keita had dissolved Mali's constitutional court in July. Ostensibly to ease tension caused by the protests calling for his resignation. Interestingly enough, parliamentary election results covering thirty seats had been overturned by that same court in April. Giving an advantage to Keita's political party. Eleven protestors were killed by security forces at the time, amid accusations of election fraud. Keita was also accused of not dealing properly with the violence caused by the rebels. Those who had joined forces with the jihadist groups. In particular, the Jama'at Nasr al-Islam wa al-Muslimin or JNIM. Whilst the political situation had been made worse by economic struggles, and volatile prices for the gold and agricultural commodities on which Mali relies. Prices had suffered a further decline because of the covid-19 global pandemic. All this at a time when nearly half of Malians were already living in extreme poverty.

The 2012 independence rebellion had also started in the Kati barracks, and quickly escalated into a full scale attempt to overthrow President Amadou Toumane Toure. Civil and political disorder followed a failed countercoup, with intervention from the international community. In 2012 Malian soldiers rioted when their demands for better weapons; ammunition, and equipment had not been met. To support them in defeating the Tuareg rebels back then. The defence minister attempted to negotiate with them, but failed to reach any agreement. So the crisis soon escalated. The original intention in 2012 had not been to overthrow the President, but this soon turned into a full scale rebellion and coup aimed at defeating the government.

Mutinies have occurred throughout the Tuaregs' struggle for independence. Not only in 2012, and with more regularity than coups against the Malian government. Both usually have dire consequences for civilians, and can escalate into severe forms of political violence. They also often indicate that a coup will follow on behind. Burkina Faso had four mutinies in 2011 then a successful coup in 2014, with an attempt at another during the following year. The question has to be asked here why some mutinies turn into coups when others do not? In Mali's case, mass political protests are an important factor. They can easily turn into a mutiny, or coup. It seems that similar protests in the capital of Bamako are also more likely to become a coup. Possibly because they are a sign that there is widespread support for this greater attempt at change. Which may in turn persuade the leadership of the mutiny or military to change their perspective, and take matters further than they may had originally intended.

The repercussions following what happened in 2020 still bear further analysis at the time of writing this book. Nevertheless there has been an adverse, international reaction to the coup. Whilst the action taken by the Tuareg rebels was yet another demand for Mali to become a true democratic state. A vital step in the cessation of human rights' violations which are happening there. After harsh criticism by the Economic Community of West African States or ECOWAS, fifteen countries closed their borders with Mali and instigated sanctions against the conspirators. The United Nations; European Union and the African Union also condemned the coup. Making those seeking to overthrow the Malian government vulnerable to the possibility of an even greater international response. Especially because of the large number of foreign troops in Mali. Eleven thousands of which had been deployed by the United Nations stabilisation mission, and an extra five thousand French soldiers. It also remains to be seen whether Aid dependence will play an important role in what happens next. The World Bank has estimated that overseas development assistance is around seventy percent of Mali's central government expenditure.

An international intervention could prove to be important in creating change, although this might be strengthened or weakened by Mali's internal dynamics. Given that there hasn't been any public support for Keita or his government, it makes his return seem unlikely. External pressure could of course change that, but the situation remains open ended at the moment. Elections usually happen after a coup, and again, this seems likely here because of international pressure. However, even if the election process itself proceeds in a proper manner, this doesn't necessarily say a great deal about the future government. Whilst allowing all interested parties to have representation in an election could lead to multiparty elections in the future, and avoid a similar 2012 experience.

By August, 20th a new military junta, the National Committee for the salvation of the People, was established in Bamako. With the promise of an election, and a situation of greater confidence between the people of Mali and the government. This has caused further alarm across the world because of its potential to have a destabilising effect on the entire region. The President of the European Council, Charles Michel, told a press conference that returning stability and the fight against terrorism needed to be treated as a priority. Similarly, the release of the prisoners, and the restoration of a state of law. He also stressed the importance of continuing the close cooperation which had been established with different African institutions, and could lead to matters being resolved in line with the aspirations of the Malian people.

Michel was not alone in voicing these concerns. Similar messages were sent out by the European Union; United States, and the Arabs. It was felt that this could easily create a situation capable of being exploited by Islamist extremists. Even though the French military had managed to rid the major towns and cities of them, they are still getting stronger. Military resources were also being used by the United States; Italy, and Germany. While the United Nations currently spends one billion euros every year in paying for its fifteen thousand soldiers. A necessary step when more than sixty percent of Mali's total area is now occupied by Azawad fighters and others. In those areas which are still controlled by the Malian government, corruption is more often than not present, causing anger and criticism from those it is supposed to represent. How can this be regarded as democratic, when it clearly is not?

The increased terrorism and current political breakdown are not surprisingly having a detrimental effect on the Tuaregs, and others currently living in Mali. Those who have already lived through conflict and resistance for many years. Millions of people in the Sahel region have become trapped by this situation, and violence has become a part of their everyday existence. As if that wasn't bad enough, the crisis has recently become worse for several reasons. Not least the coronavirus pandemic. Violence within the region has escalated since the start of the pandemic. Increasing the death rate; injuries suffered, and displacement of the Tuareg people and others. The impact on health facilities has been huge. Eighteen percent of those in Mali have been destroyed. Ninety percent of which are in the north.

I can understand why this latest coup happened. My people have simply been trying to survive for too long whilst subject to continual repression. The president whom they had again been asked to trust in looking after their interests, and even improve the situation for them, quickly became corrupt like so many others before him. This pattern has to change! President Keita was elected in September, 2013 following the failure of the Azawad declaration of independence. With the jihadists overrunning parts of the north and central Mali, earlier that year. Keita was obviously expected to do whatever was necessary to get

Mali back on its feet again. So that everyone could finally move on from what had happened.

Instead he revealed himself to be an inept leader, becoming involved in a number of intrigues which had been at the heart of Malian politics for years. Coupled with a fiscal crisis, and other problems. His answer to the problem was to buy a presidential aeroplane not long after he was inaugurated! His friends and associates were given positions of authority, without any regard to their lack of qualifications. His son, Karim, who became well known for his lavish lifestyle was rewarded by being appointed chairman of the government's defence committee. Until he resigned from this position in August. Meanwhile, the violation of the Tuaregs' human rights increased along with their suffering. A leaked report from the United Nations also revealed that drug traffickers were actively present in Mali. Some of which served high placed cliques in Bamako!

Keita's answer was not to focus on urgent issues like this. He chose instead to abuse Mali's political institutions. Like the constitutional Court which decides on the validity of election results, and the national assembly. Presumably in an attempt to consolidate his monopoly of power. All this came to a head in early 2020, following protests against him, and the M5 movement which formed later in June. Its intention was to remove the president's power of harming the state any further, and start a series of reforms which would culminate in Mali's resurrection. However well meaning this might have seemed, those who were involved in the movement were also not beyond criticism. The main participant was Mahmoud Dicko, an uncompromising adherent of the salafi, or strict Sunni Muslim sect. It had already destroyed a law in 2009 designed to increase the autonomy of women, and later opposed the introduction of sex education in schools as a possible means of promoting homophobia.

Another problem for the movement in opposing Keita was that he still had three years left of his five year term of office. As a result, he held constitutional legitimacy. Despite this the protests continued throughout the summer months, focused on Keita's resignation. There were between eleven and twenty three fatalities, and although concessions were made by the President, these were rejected. Subsequent mediation by ECOWAS also failed to break the impasse which had arisen. When the coup happened, it actually caused very little damage to the people there at the time. Apart from forcing Keita to resign, and making a further election likely with a transitional government being put in place in the meantime. Unfortunately, this is unlikely to provide an answer to the root of the problem faced by the Tuareg people seeking to establish a true democracy in Mali. Dicko and others in the M5 movement also have their own agenda.

The main problem remains the considerable abuse of political institutions, which has existed in the west African Francophile states since 1960, and the ongoing practice of quite simply breaking the rules. When politicians like Keita can sabotage democracy from within. In the repeated coups which follow, the participants invariably return to this ongoing violation of democracy. Simply following the pattern set by their predecessors

There are many examples of this including the Ivory Coast's president, Alassane Ouattara, recently declaring his intention to break yet another constitutional rule. Of being in office for only two consecutive terms, and a candidate for his own succession later this year. Whilst Alpha Conde, President of Guinea, has followed a similar path. Although Mahamadou Issoufou in Niger has said that he will not break the two term rule, he has altered electoral rules to marginalise the opposition. The President of Burkina Faso, Roch Marc Christian Kabore, so far remains the exception to the case.

The political situation in Mali is ominous. The Tuareg people are not the only ones concerned about how it will ultimately be resolved. Given the rise of the jihadist groups, this will play a vital part in the security of the Sahel and beyond. All of us need to do what we can, to ensure that peace is the ultimate outcome of this latest coup. Ending the violence and devastation throughout the region. The democratic sham in Mali has been at the heart of this ongoing problem for far too long.

Photographs

Tuareg children attending the Inetalan school in Sebha. Most of whom had left their families in the Sahara, to receive an education and military training in Colonel Qadafi's camps.

Other Tuareg children in one of Colonel Qadafi's camps.

Toumast Broadcasting Image received in Libya.

Akli Sh'kka (middle), Ayoub Ag Chamed (right), and Mustafa Ag Azawi (left) at the Toumast Studio in Paris.

A monument at the centre of Kidal, symbolising Tuareg independence in 2012 and victory for Azawad.

Another monument in Kidal, celebrating Tuareg independence in 2012.

Akli Sh'kka (front) taking part in a peaceful demonstration during 2013 outside the French Embassy in London, against France's intervention in Azawad.

A second photograph of the 2013 demonstration in London.

A third photograph of the 2013 demonstration in London.

An Azawad protest against the United Nations' presence in Kidal during 2015.

Tuareg Cameleers carrying the Azawad flag, following the declaration of independence in 2012.

Akli Sh'kka in Kidal during 2019.

Libya: Tuareg members of "No for Racism Movement", Ubari
(southern Libya), 2020

Libya: "No for racism Movement" activist writing on the wall along with movement's motto

Libya: "No for Racism Movement" activists protesting against the systematic discrimination

Libya: "No for Racism Movement" Tuareg children holing Libyan flag along with the movement's logo

Libya: "No for Racism Movement" student activists

Azawad independence supporters protesting in Kidal 2017

Mali: General Alhaji Ag Gamou with his GATIA fighters

Azawad children holding Azawad flag

MNLA's Fighters at one of the Movement's training camps, Kidal

MNLA's children supporters wearing T-shirts with Azawad flag, Kidal

Akli Sh'kka surrounded by MNL's fighters, Kidal 2019

Chapter 9

Comparing The Tuaregs In Mali With Those Elsewhere

As a means of evaluating whether there could be any other reasons for the failure of Azawad in 2012, and why the Tuaregs in Mali have rebelled on so many occasions across the years, I believe it is important to compare them to those living in other neighbouring countries. Such as Libya; Niger, and Algeria. To ascertain the political; social, and economic differences which could have contributed to this.

The national uprisings which have swept across most of north Africa and the Levant since late 2011 spread into parts of the Sahara. These sudden political changes resulted in the toppling of undemocratic regimes like those in Tunisia, and Libya. Where a large percentage of the Tuareg people had settled, or had become part of the Libyan army for many years. But the course of events changed suddenly after Qaddafi's death and the collapse of his regime in October, 2011. Due to these rapid political changes in Libya and other parts of the region, hundreds of heavily armed Tuareg rebels who had been fighting for Qaddafi or the Libyan rebels, started making their way home to northern Mali. This seemed at the time even more likely to happen because of the intensification of NATO's air strikes against the Qaddafi regime during August and September, 2011.

Ibrahim Ag Bahanga, the leader of the May Alliance, had been in Libya since 2009. Following peace agreements signed with the Malian government. According to sources close to him, Ag Bahanga and other Tuareg officers who had been serving in the Libyan military for a number of years, managed to secretly mobilise a large number of men and stockpiles of ammunition from Qaddafi's military supplies. Sending them to northern Mali, between August and September, 2011. Earlier in July, Bahanga also managed to make his way to the Zakak Mountains, again in the far north of Mali. Accompanied by at least five hundred men. The majority of whom had defected from the thirty second brigade. Led by Qaddafi's son Khamis, and the Maghawir Brigade, by General Ali Kanna. Soon after his arrival in the area, Bahanga began to prepare his fighters for combat against the Malian government. Aiming, and zero pointing, his guns at the Malian positions inside their military encampments.

Suspicious circumstances have been linked to Ag Bahanga's death in a car accident on August 26, 2011. His relatives and friends still believe that this was a planned execution carried out by Islamist radical groups. Some of whom were close to the Algerian security service. Whilst the facts remain elusive it is equally possible that if he did die in an accident, this was whilst he was in pursuit of another vehicle. Controlling the trade in weapons, and trafficking of illegal drugs. We know now that when he was in Libya, Ag Bahanga refused Qaddafi's order to push forward into Azawaya and Misurata where fierce fighting was continuing against the Libyans. Instead of doing this he accumulated weapons and ammunition, to liberate his own country from the Malian presence, but his death had prevented this ambition from being realised.

By the end of August, 2011 the Zakaka Mountains in northern Mali were however swarming with hundreds of Tuareg fighters who had been pouring in from the south. Soldiers who had deserted from the Libyan army. It seems likely that the total number of Tuareg fighters who returned from Libya between March and October was at least three thousand. Most of them wishing to seize the opportunity, to make their long term dream of Azawad a reality.

The fall of Qaddafi's regime in 2011 also had another important effect. It resulted in approximately two hundred and fifty thousand Tuaregs in Libya insisting more vehemently on being given their human rights. The Colonel's policy had been to control others by keeping them in need. Sometimes he would grant rights to specific individuals, but not whole communities. For example non-Arab minorities in Sebha, including the Tuaregs, suffered from political and cultural marginalisation.The regime followed a pan-Arabic ideology so refused to recognise my people as a distinct indigenous group.

Since Qaddafi's fall, several associations have formed in Tayuri to promote the rights of the Tuaregs living there. According to the International Crisis Group for North Africa the arabisation of minority groups, including the Tuaregs, had advanced more quickly in Libya than any other Maghreb country. The Tuaregs living in Libya were legally forbidden from giving their children non-Arab names, and if they were found to have attended cultural celebrations in neighbouring countries were arrested on their return. Even those who had been absorbed into Qaddafi's army suffered from this marginalisation.

Although there was a sense of optimism for some when the Qaddafi regime ended, regarding the possibility of freedom, those living in Tayuri said that conditions remained unacceptable. When compared to other neighbourhoods in Sebha, the homes in this area had been arranged haphazardly. The Tuareg communities who lived there received little help from the state. There wasn't a proper sewage or refuse disposal system in place for them to use. The lack of infrastructure in the area, and adherence to safety regulations had caused a lot of problems. Like the electric cables scattered on the ground in between the houses. These caused a number of infant deaths from electric shock when the children played outside.

The United Nations Refugee Agency or UNHCR reported at the time that the poverty in Tayuri, and other Tuareg neighbourhoods, exceeded that in the rest of Libya. My people had to build the houses themselves, and many were suffering from hunger. They were unable to register their children at school which became a problem later for the Tuareg youth. Whilst those who did carry on studying to University level found it difficult to get good jobs. Putting them in the same category as the illiterate Tuaregs who hadn't been able to go to school. This was obviously demoralising, and in some cases, led to a lack of motivation in trying to do anything else.

As I mentioned in an earlier chapter, the Tuaregs in Libya were denied official documentation proving their citizenship. This was usually a booklet in which all of the family members were listed. It was required when applying for jobs; university places; scholarships, or taking out a bank loan. Tuareg families in Libya for one hundred years had managed to get these documents, but those who settled there even fifty years ago were refused them. As a result many remained without Libyan, or other citizenship. This prevented them from travelling to study; get medical treatment outside Libya, become a high ranking officer in the army or government, and buy property. The situation essentially made the Tuaregs in Libya a stateless minority. Yet another political, legal, and administrative issue which remains unresolved. A far cry from the Tuaregs who were recognised historically as an independent nation, living in their own homeland on the sands of the *Tenere* desert, part of the area declared as Azawad in 2012.

The independence activists in Tayuri who approached Libya's National Transition Council or NTC, after the fall of Qaddafi's regime, were told that citizenship for those who had their origins in Libya would be considered after the elections. Needless to say this was not done, and the question as to who is a true Libyan still has the potential to become an explosive issue. As I have said before, the Imazighen or Tuaregs are the original people of Libya from centuries ago. That alone gives them the moral right to be regarded as a Libyan. It is notable here, due again to innate corruption and elements of self interest in the Libyan government, the stance taken by them is that the original Libyan is someone who speaks Arabic!

Another major disadvantage for the Tuaregs who didn't have a family booklet was that they were unable to register to vote in the 2012 Libyan elections. Which was again another democratic issue, following the Azawad independence declaration. In an attempt to resolve the problem, the government did eventually allow those with an alternative family document, as well as a driver's licence or national identity card, to register.

The ongoing possibility remains that even if official documents are given to all of my people, these might not be the same as those held by other Libyans. A situation which would of course continue to perpetrate the discrimination against them. It is also notable that those without documents cannot run for political office, and are therefore prevented from seeking a change for the better through these channels.

Whilst in Niger after the fall of Qaddafi's regime, the number of Tuareg men and women who returned from Libya was less than two hundred. This considerable difference in number could well be one of the underlying reasons for the Tuareg in Niger not revolting against their government when those in Mali did. The government in Niger was in a far better position to handle the smaller number returning from the Libyan war. The majority of whom were not soldiers. Even those who did go back with weapons were quickly disarmed by the government. Whereas in Mali the situation proved again to be very different.

Whenever a rebellion had occurred historically in northern Mali, another happened at the same time in the north of Niger and vice versa. Moreover until recently Tuareg rebel leaders in Niger and Mali believed that their cause; grievances, and ambitions for a united homeland were the same. Their respective countries treated them with the same level of animosity, and relegation.

During the 1990s, Tuaregs in both Mali and Niger created a combined armed front called, The Liberation Front of Aïr and Azawad or FLAA. Since the first rebellion in this decade Tuareg fighters in Niger fought alongside their Tuareg brothers in Mali and vice versa against the two governments. In July, 2007 the Tuaregs in both Niger and Mali established a new alliance, the Alliance of Tuareg in Niger and Mali for Change. The leaders of this new movement had a goal. To liberate the Tuareg traditional lands in northern Niger (Aïr-Azawagh), and northern Mali (Azawad), from occupational forces controlled by the two national governments. This movement did not survive for long, but almost succeeded in organising offensive attacks in both Mali and Niger. Before the Tuareg people in those countries reached peace agreements in Algeria during 1991 with their respective governments. The Tuaregs in Niger also joined, and provided military and logistic support to their brothers in Mali, during their short lived rebellion in the mid-2000s.

Whilst the level of grievances in Mali appear to be much higher than those of the Tuaregs in Niger, they still exist. Despite the Tuaregs in Niger not taking up arms against their government in 2012 when the call for the independence of Azawad was made, there is considerable evidence of them suffering from discrimination. With the destruction of their culture, and former way of life. Nevertheless there are still other differences which may have been at the root of their decision not to rebel.

The government in Niger had successfully included many Tuaregs into its state system, and had been more positive about implementing the previous peace agreements signed by Tuareg leaders. Whereas the situation in Mali was essentially the opposite. Most of the political agreements that were signed after the second rebellion in 1990, between the Tuaregs and Malian government, ended up on the shelves of Bamako. Only to be retrieved when another rebellion erupted.

In 2007, the Nigerian government signed a peace agreement with the Tuareg leaders of Le Mouvement Des Nigériens Pour La Justice or MNJ. This was done under mediation by Colonel Qaddafi. As part of this agreement he promised the rebels compensation in 2009 on behalf of the Nigerian government. But it is common knowledge that these promises were not kept. France was believed to have used part of Areva's uranium revenue to bribe the Tuareg leaders with cash. So that they would remain silent about their earlier hostile stance towards the company's activities in the area.

Niger had also shown an interest in consolidating its citizens, and the government rapidly took measures to implement the peace agreement signed in 2007. It also made great strides in ending centralisation, by integrating ex-soldiers into the army; police, and society in general. Most importantly, the government provided a fair percentage of its natural resources for the local Tuareg population in the north. Where the Areva company had been extracting uranium for more than forty-five years. Although it took quite a long time to happen, the government also began to allocate a proportion of the proceeds of the company's production, to build up the infrastructure in Tuareg areas. In places like Agadez; Arlit, and Tahoua. The government also promoted substantial medium sized projects, honouring their commitment to do so.

Most of the Tuareg rebel leaders in Niger today hold senior positions in the government. For instance the prime minister of Niger, Brigi Rafini, is a Tuareg who has held this position since 2011. Also, the Niger government which supported decentralisation, has allowed the northern part of the country to operate its own self-government and be led by traditional local representatives. Whilst the Tuareg situation in Mali remains far less satisfactory. As you have already seen in earlier chapters of this book, successive Malian governments have not been quite so positive about meeting the Tuaregs' political expectations. Most of the agreements signed by Tuareg rebels and the Malian governments since the 1990s and in 2009, are not worth the paper they were written on. Many Tuareg leaders remain worried that this could easily happen again to the 2015 accords signed in Algeria.

The global coronavirus pandemic in 2020 has resulted in a regional lockdown of frontiers and trade routes, successfully preventing all trade in the Sahel region. Apart from the growing hunger and starvation which this has created, the worst consequence has been the many serious violations of human rights. Atrocities which have been taking place against the Tuareg and Fulani people in Niger. Earlier in the year, more than thirty six of my people were killed by the Nigerian Army at Ayarou and in the Tera areas. One of the victims was called Abdulaye. He was twenty seven years old when he was murdered by the Nigerian army soldiers near Tellabere. A Fulani herder, he was tied up and shot along with his animals, before military tanks ran over their bodies. The Nigerian government's only comment was that its army had killed a number of terrorists in the area that day.

This dismissive version of the truth has since been refuted by both local civilians, and Human Rights bodies including the Imouhagh International Organization for Justice and Transparency. The latter is well-informed, and concerns itself with the whole region. It has published a formal letter, demanding a thorough investigation into the incident by the Nigerian government. Followed by impartial justice being granted to the families of those innocent victims who had been murdered by the Nigerian army.

Another victim, in a different post-colonial state, was Attyoub Ag Allou. He was forty years old, and the father of six children. Completely dependent on UNHCR support for survival he was living at Mentao Refugee Camp in the province of Djibo, Burkina Faso. This man was arrested before being tied up in front of members of his family, and severely beaten. He survived to tell the tale, after managing to escape a few days later from the place where he was being held. A second victim from the same refugee camp at Mentao was less fortunate. He was a sixty year old blind man who had been hired by the camp residents to look after their animals. He was murdered later in front of his family.

The question must again be asked why the Tuaregs in these regions have not revolted against their governments. Especially when atrocities and human rights violations like this are regularly taking place. It is possible that one of the main reasons why the Tuareg people in Algeria and Libya have never raised arms is because they consider themselves as part of the North African community. Or Berber-Amazigh nation. Having an identity, and culture, similar to the Tuaregs in Mali.

Moreover, both the Tuaregs in Algeria and Libya have until recently been able to control their lands, without direct interference from their respective governments. Whilst the situation in Niger and Mali is the opposite to this. The Arabs and Tuaregs in those countries believe there is a huge gap between the black Africans and them. This extends from race to culture; identity; traditional customs relating to land, and language. Being very similar to what Samuel Huntington describes as, a clash of cultures.

This isn't to say that the situation is entirely satisfactory. Algeria's Tuareg population in the Tamanrasset wilaya region, and possibly other areas, were again demonstrating their unhappiness during 2018. In relation to the way they were being treated by the authorities. This did not however lead to a coup. I believe that it goes back to the time when Algeria was being given its independence by France in 1962, and what was being said then about Algeria's "Tuareg problem." Concerning essentially the degree of ethnic tension between the government, and those indigenous Tuaregs of the southern desert regions who were living in Algeria. Most notably the Ahaggar massif and the Tassili-n-Ajjer which cover around twenty percent of the country. Including the majority of the Tamanghasset and Illizi.

The Tuareg problem is similar to the Berber question in northern Algeria which also exists today. Given that the Tuaregs are a Berber or Amazigh people. The exact number of Tuaregs in Algeria is unknown. Language surveys in the latter part of the twentieth century indicated that those speaking Tamahaq, the language of the northern Tuaregs, were twenty five thousand. Twenty thousand of which were in Ahaggar (Tamanghasset) and five thousand in Ajjer (Illizi). Whilst national censuses do not differentiate ethnic identities, it was estimated that the population then was more than fifty thousand. This could however be greater if the number of Nigerian and Malian Tuaregs in the region are included.

The latter group of Tuaregs consider that they are being marginalised. One of the reasons for this was because Tamanghasset's urban population almost doubled in the 1990s. When northern Algerians sought refuge there with their families, from the civil war in the north. In 2000 the population of Tamanghasset, which had previously only been four thousand in 2012, had grown to one hundred thousand. As a result the Tuaregs became a small minority in their own region which naturally led to a lot of frustration and anger. Algeria has also suffered from corruption in its successive governments. Since President Abdelaziz Bouteflika came to power in the Tamanghasset area during 1999, poor governance and this have been rife. Especially towards the Tuareg population.

It is a sad truth that former governments in Mali have shown scant interest in meeting their obligations set out in earlier peace agreements. At the same time, continually accusing the Tuareg rebels of evading their responsibilities, and being difficult to integrate into Malian society. The level of corruption in Mali was far higher in 2012 and now, than in any of its other neighbouring countries. It runs deep through the respective governments; armies, and infrastructure of each country. It is also inherently linked to the use of terrorist groups in securing funding from foreign countries, which helps to enable the current status quo to continue. Since 2012, with the exception of Mali, the respective governments have taken measures to alleviate the problem. Albeit to a lesser or greater extent.

However, change is obviously still necessary. The atrocities and violation of human rights I have described in this chapter and elsewhere cannot be allowed to continue. And there have been so many others which I haven't been able to include. The effect of the covid virus on the whole of West Africa also remains to be seen. Many deaths have already been predicted. Terrorist groups are seizing the opportunity to hand out food and money to people in exchange for their loyalty, and a promise of joining the organisation. Criminal gangs and terrorist groups are active, and flourishing. Particularly in the vicinity of Tellabere, Inaker, and Menka. In April, 2020 according to eye witness reports, the fundamentalist Islamic State in the Greater Sahara had started to lure even more young people into their ranks. This group goes back to 2015, and is led by Abu Walid al-Sahraoui.

One of the organization's recruiting agents was seen near Menka and Inaker. Distributing both food, and cash to some of the poorest families which have suffered the most. The same agent is one of the organisation's most active local leaders. According to one source he had managed to recruit at least thirty five young men in this area. Another member of the same terrorist organisation appeared to have a similar assignment, and recruiting mission in the Tellabere region. Close to a small village near the border between western Niger and Mali. Recruitment activity is thought to have increased tenfold since April 13th, 2020. When many countries in the Sahel region closed their national borders in an attempt to restrict the pandemic.

Looking at the situation as a whole, Azawad must not be forgotten. Peace will not become a reality for my people, especially in the north and I will repeat it again here, unless they gain their independence. At the very least, an autonomy or some form of federalisation, to enable them to have better lives. With an equitable share in the distribution of power, and vast resources of the region.

Chapter 10

The Effect Of The Algiers 2015 Peace Accords

The Algiers' Accords between the government of Mali and different factions of the Azawad independence movements were signed during May, 2015. Five years later, I can confidently say that this is still far from the end of the matter.

This sentiment was expressed earlier by the Azawad Liberation Movement's Secretary General, Bilal Ag Achareef, during an interview with Al-Qudas Al-Arabi newspaper. He said that whilst the question of Azawad has not been properly addressed, there would not be stability in the Sahel region. He blamed the failure of Azawad on the weak role played by the international community. Namely, the United Nations, and the European Union. Together with the more active role of regional countries like Niger; Algeria, and Libya. In disregarding the old, deeply rooted, political problems of the people of northern Mali. The Tuaregs, and that this was done by conflating their legitimate political demands with terrorism. He criticised the French in particular for taking the same perspective as the Malian government on the question of the north. Believing that this approach would make the situation even more complicated.

Despite intense regional and international political mediation the two main opposing parties, the Malian government and the Coordination of Movements of Azawad or CMA, have so far not been persuaded to keep the promises they made in Algiers during 2015. When a peace deal was negotiated, after eight months of sporadic negotiations, and pitfalls on both sides. The thirty page peace agreement respects Mali's territorial integrity, and takes account of its ethnic and cultural diversity. Whilst also giving the Tuareg rebels semi-autonomy, and with greater representation of the northern populations in national institutions. Also the means of transferring thirty percent of budget revenue to local authorities in the north. Given that there has not been any significant progress in implementing the agreement, it may not be unreasonable to conclude that we appear to be back at square one. Apart from the change brought by the 2012 rebellion in respect of our having had public support on social media; television, and radio to a certain extent.

Whilst the agreement fails to be implemented, there has been a high risk of the hostilities between the CMA and Malian army being renewed. Supported by different armed groups. Most notably GATIA; Ganda Koy, and Ganda Izo. This challenge increased in the absence of a strong, elected government. It could even be said that Mali was still in a process of transition following the coup d'état in March, 2012 when the latest one took place.

The question remains whether an army and police presence in the north could well pose the greatest challenge to implementing the peace deal, or if the absence of this and spread of different armed groups remain likely to destabilise the area even further. Without the benefit of a proper democratic intervention, and means of dealing with corruption. These groups include the Azawad Liberation Movements who continue to seek an independent Tuareg state; terrorist groups; trafficking groups; ethnic, and tribal based militias. In a report on Mali released during May, 2016 the Secretary General of the United Nations expressed concern over the future and progress of the Algiers peace agreement. Also acknowledging that the challenges for the implementation of the agreement were daunting, and that progress made at that time had been uneven.

I still have grave concerns regarding the future of the Algiers peace deal. Ultimately how it can be sustained for a long lasting solution. I believe that the Malian government can be strongly criticised for its delay in the implementation of the 2015 peace agreement, and inherent belief that it will fail. As its predecessors did in 1990; 1992; 2006, and so on. The situation has been made more complex by the propagation of different armed groups with various divisions; the rise of ethnic violence, and tensions between the groups with their own ideologies. The terrorist groups; and national, and political movements. All vying for different gains, add more weight to the historical challenges we were already facing. There is now the spread of arms; national, and transnational organised crimes that need to be considered as part of the problem. Including drug trafficking; arms; cigarettes, and illegal migration. Let alone the absence of a strong, and unified national army in the north. Not of course forgetting to mention the effects of the 2020 coup which still remain to be seen.

When I began writing this book it was based only on the 2012 bid for the creation of a new, independent, state called Azawad. The number of things which had contributed to the failure of the project. By looking more closely at the reasons and what actually happened, this appeared at first glance to turn the overview of the situation I had taken into an utter fiasco. That our dream of a Tuareg state called Azawad had been completely quashed for the foreseeable future. But a spark of light does remain, and I soon began to ask myself whether this was really the end of Azawad. Our hope and dream of an independent state.

When the so-called Arab Spring swept through the Sahara in 2011, the majority of the Libyan based Tuaregs chose to side with their long term "rescuer" and intermittent patron, Qaddafi. They were opposed to another Arab revolution in Libya. They feared that this might guarantee permanent subordination to their long term oppressors, the far more numerous Arabs. To give themselves a greater chance of survival, they bided their time. That choice eventually provided them with a number of remarkable opportunities, to strengthen their prospects. With the fall of the Qadafi state, they gained access to a considerable amount of cash, as well as modern and sophisticated weaponry. So that they soon felt strong enough to embark on the 2012 rebellion. In pursuit of full autonomy and control of their own state in the northern part of Mali, following a declaration of its independence.

This is an example of the spirit of the Tuareg people of whom I am honoured to be a part, and whose ancestors have walked the sands of the Tenere for millenia. So the answer to my question is... No! It is not time to relinquish all hope, of a better future for our families and ourselves. We have yet to see the effects of the latest coup on 18th August, 2020. Whilst I believe, the future belongs to all of us. Azawad remains... As do the Tuaregs.

Chapter 11

Toumast And The Influence Of The Media On Our Independence

I was born during 1983 in the Sahara desert. My father was a herder and, like a lot of other Tuareg men, he travelled on the back of a camel. Going away on business for weeks at a time. As I was too young to go with him, I was left behind with my brothers; sisters, and our mother who looked after us. She taught us the old ways of the Amazigh people, and in our culture, the Tifinagh scriptures which are learned before anything else. I remember it as a good time, with evenings spent by the fire. Learning to write in the sand, and absorbing many new words from the Tamasheq language.

This nomadic way of life changed when I was six or seven years old, and my family decided to join those who went to Libya. Following Colonel Qaddafi's promise of a much better way of life for the Tuareg people. We settled in the Elttayori camp in Sebha, seven hundred kilometers south of Tripoli. Sebha is the capital of Fezzan in southwest Libya and which, according to tradition, is the place where the Tuareg people originated. I learned of this from the stories which others told about the Tuaregs' nomadic life. Sadly, the move to Libya was not as most of us had expected, and the situation there today has deteriorated even further. Sebha itself has now become one of the most lawless areas in Libya.

My family and I became outcasts in what I can only describe as a ghetto, with dire conditions. Three hundred families lived inside this camp, making a few thousand people in total. It saddens me to think that some still live there in abject poverty. We were truly fortunate to be able to leave.

There was only one well that we could drink from. No proper system in place for the disposal of sewage. The houses were made of earth, and as you know, Colonel Qaddafi didn't have any intention of keeping his promises to those who went to Libya. I did however manage to attend school while I was there.

By the time I was fifteen years old, my friends and I realised that as Tuaregs we belonged to a minority of people who were being discriminated against. We were growing up in an environment where bullying, based on our ethnicity and origins, had become part of daily life. Simply because we were "Tuaregs." When we spoke the Arabs laughed at us, and I am reluctant even now to call myself a citizen of Libya.

In an attempt to do something to alleviate the situation, a friend and I began secretly to make a film in 2007. In the hope that others across the world might be able to see the conditions in which the Tuaregs, and their families, were living. Or put another way, struggling to survive. Another friend who was working in Saudi Arabia promised to find ways of broadcasting it. So that we could spread our message by showcasing, and interviewing, some of the inhabitants of the region talking to us. We asked them simple questions. What did they think of their living conditions? Why didn't they leave? An older man likened his situation to being trapped by the authorities, *as camels in a swamp*. In the cities he told us that they would have had to fight against the police, and discrimination. Whilst their only adversary in the desert was Nature herself. The inference being that this was how it should be, if all was right with the world. Not as they were expected to live back then.

After this, like so many other young Tuaregs, it quickly became apparent that I would have to leave Libya and go into exile. I chose England for my new home. When I arrived in Yorkshire during 2009 the majority of people there didn't know anything about us. Or what was happening to the Tuaregs in Africa. Other than possibly having an early twentieth century image spring to mind of a man on a camel. Riding majestically through the desert on his way to Tinbuktu. A place which they, or someone they knew, might have visited as a tourist while it was still possible to do this. When that couldn't now be further from the truth. As you will have seen from reading this book.

I stayed in Halifax for five years. Volunteering as an interpreter for the Red Cross, and during that time I talked about my culture. Life in the Sahara. I also managed to edit the film we had secretly made, and called this twenty-seven minute documentary: *Imshuradj, A People Without Country*. It was screened at several festivals. I have included a link to it at the end of the book on my Author page. So that you can watch it, if you would like to.

After that I went on to create Tifinagh, an association which aimed to teach Tuareg history and culture to others. Its name is related to the ancient Tuareg script or form of writing that goes back thousands of years to around 3,000 BC. I received help from my new friends in Halifax, Daniel Russell, John Hellewell family and John Gaukroger, who respectively became secretary and treasurer of the association. And I know I speak for other Tuaregs when I say this. Although we may have left the Tenere, a part of it came with us to the safety of the United Kingdom, and the other countries where some of us now live. We are truly fortunate. When so many other Tuaregs are still suffering a violation of their human rights, and struggling to survive.

In 2012, I established The Imouhagh International Organisation for the Sake of Justice and Transparency. Its aim is to embody the voice of all Tuaregs at an international level. To ensure that a single powerful, and legitimate, voice can speak on behalf of all of the Tuareg people wherever they might be. Also, to gain access to higher levels of international decision making. As well as the most crucial governmental, and non-governmental, organisations.

Following this and with the encouragement of others, I became a political commentator on the BBC; Al Jazeera, and France 24. Analysing the situation in Libya, and the failure of Azawad. To support the overthrow of the Qaddafi regime which had by this time lasted forty years. Also, the much needed democratic change, and I was soon being interviewed by the media on a daily basis. When Mali was affected by the war in 2012, I was asked to be there to represent the Tuareg youth movement, and I was honoured to defend the rights of my people. In particular in July of that year, when those who were responsible for the destruction of the Timbuktu tombs in Azawad were placed on trial.

In 2015 I played a part in the tribal war which took place between the Tuaregs, and Black African Toubou people from the south of the Sahara. Thankfully, we were able to initiate a peace campaign. A sustained attempt to stop the fighting, and call upon the tribes and the Toubou to lay down their arms. With a view to coming together peacefully for negotiations. I am delighted to say that this proved to be successful. The calls for peace were heard, and they found support. Or at the very least consent on both sides of those involved in the conflict. I was chosen to lead the first of two rounds of peaceful negotiations between the conflicting tribes. The talks took place in Qatar under the supervision of the Qatar Foreign Minister, Sheikh Mohammed bin Abdulrahman bin Jassim Al Thani. A month of continual negotiations led to the declaration of a ceasefire. A beneficial agreement was signed, and subsequently implemented by both parties. The terms are still being adhered to.

The alleviation of the Tuaregs' suffering can sometimes

seem to be an impossible task, but then I don't believe in giving up. Taking it one step at a time if need be, and whilst all this was going on, another idea had started to take shape. My friends and I realised that it would be beneficial for the Tuaregs to have their own communication channel. A radio station which would be accessible, via the internet. Followed by a television channel. Both of which would require funding. Lots of it. But due to my ongoing involvement with the media and in human rights cases, I was aware of the extraordinary influence which the media could have on people's lives; thoughts, and beliefs. So perhaps this might be the means of bringing a substantial change for the better?

It led to the inception of an internet radio operation in our own language, Tamasheq. My friends and I spoke about it at length. We all thought it could be a good way of getting innocent Tuaregs to be more wary of becoming involved in terrorist activities. To show them through a variety of programmes what was actually happening in the Sahara. That they would be best advised to distance themselves from the truly dangerous, bad guys who had arrived. Mostly ISIS, and Al Qaeda. We thought that using radio to get this message across to them would be a good start. It soon became apparent however that the internet was not readily available to enough of the nomadic Tuareg people. Not many would be able to listen to V.I.R. broadcasts. So what we had set out to do wasn't going to work! Despite the great mixture of popular North African music we had in mind. Along with informative and educational; news, and talk programmes.

Meanwhile, all of us were becoming increasingly concerned about the Islamic terrorism that was increasing rapidly day by day. Especially because of our people's perceived laxity in practising the Islamic faith. The unusually high respect for women within our traditional culture, and that they are able to hold elevated positions in society. Again, giving up wasn't an option, and another campaign was organised to help the Tuareg people. Using our internet radio service, Voice of Imouhagh, and social media. I posted on my personal Facebook page; Youtube, and Whatsapp groups. We called on the Tuareg elders throughout the Sahara, and the educated Tuareg youth, to help us establish a dedicated television channel. A discussion group on Viber, and Whatsapp was created. The group brought together around sixty Tuaregs from Algeria; Niger; Mali; Libya, and the diaspora. Together we considered how the necessary funds might be raised. Everyone became responsible for addressing a certain group, and convincing them of the viability of the project.

By then the word was spreading, and a lot of Tuaregs knew who I was from my public profile. I had a good reputation so others began to trust me. The fundraising worked beyond our wildest dreams. In six months, the sixty Tuaregs and I had raised the money we needed. Following this cry for help, hundreds of Tuareg volunteers in Libya; Niger; Algeria; Azawad (Mali), and around Europe collected donations and contributions to pay for it.

Several television groups in the region were contacted, and all of them agreed to our proposal for a new channel. Especially since the money was there to pay for it! This led to us entering into an agreement with NileSat, the satellite which broadcasts in north Africa and the Sahara. We had then to think about recruiting the staff we needed. I was a little concerned at first. Not knowing whether I would find the right people to help us, but as it turned out we were spoiled for choice. Almost every Tuareg who found out about the project wanted to be a part of it.

Toumast TV was created in July, 2014. With two hours of live broadcasting every day, and the remainder of the programmes, pre-recorded. Around fifty people were working on its twenty-four hour broadcasting schedule from

Libya; Niger; the Azawad region; France, and even discreetly, Algeria. During the first three months of production, Toumast had up to thirty million viewers. Either in the Sahara; other parts of North Africa, or Europe. The team and I received around six thousand congratulatory texts every day. So that Toumast soon became the most popular channel in the Sahara, and north Africa.

As part of its flagship programme 'Asihar Dagh Paris' which can be translated as direct from Paris, internationally renowned groups like Tinariwen who won a Grammy Award in 2012 were invited to perform. Abdallah, the manager of the group, remembers how he felt as a viewer... That as Tuaregs, we still had hope. Something which many had stopped believing was possible, and Toumast was their inspiration.

Unfortunately, neighbouring countries like Algeria found it difficult to accept that the Tuareg people had a voice of their own. One that could be heard, and so might become influential. We quickly began having problems. The war in southern Libya caught up with us. During October, 2014 the Toumast TV located in the town of Oubari was attacked by a rocket. On the edge of Fezzan and at the center of trafficking routes, Oubari had the reputation of being a stronghold for the jihadists, and the TV studio was destroyed. Attyp Issa, the head of Toumast in Oubari, was killed after being taken prisoner and tortured. Of course, all of us knew that it was going to be dangerous. But we had tried to prepare for any reprisals by decentralising our activities. After the attack happened it became even more important that several people were contributing to the Toumast broadcasts from outside the studio. Using their own computers. We hoped that this would lessen the possibility of loss of life or other reprisals in the future, and meant that the loss of the studio didn't stop us from carrying on.

The Toumast team and I had to adapt quickly. We decided to open portable studios in Tripoli, the Libyan capital, and elsewhere. Also, another at Kidal in northern Mali, and Paris in a building which had been rented out to an Algerian opposition television channel. Everything seemed to be back to normal when the fatal blow struck. Again, from Libya where salaries were no longer being paid, and banks closing, Consequently the Libyans, who represented the majority of Toumast subscribers, could no longer pay their monthly subscriptions. Even though they still had the money to do so, they were denied access to it. The Toumast team and I managed to borrow money from those around us, and we held on for another seven months. But due to lack of funding, we had finally to stop broadcasting during the summer of 2016.

The Algerian government had also taken action against us when the channel was live. Firstly, blocking the SMS texts we had been receiving from Algeria. Pressure was then exerted on the Toumast station's administration in an attempt to close us down. When the Algerians failed to get anywhere with these tactics they complained about NileSat, and demanded that this satellite be closed down. Toumast was obliged to stop using NileSat because of ongoing pressure, but was able to switch to broadcasting temporarily through a different satellite, Eutelsat.

Many people were saddened by the closure. Some had named their children after Toumast. We were equally honoured that hundreds of poems were composed about it, and songs performed by famous Tuareg bands like Tinariwen. Many of which were based on the work we had been doing to help the Tuareg people. I also believe that the success of Toumast TV can be attributed to the variety of programmes which were broadcast in the Tamasheq language. The only universal language which all Tuareg people speak. Even if some might also use others like Arabic, and French. The chief purpose of the channel remained the same throughout, to educate and enlighten the Tuareg people. With particular emphasis on combating the new wave of terrorism, which still threatens our uniquely precious and ancient culture today. As well as the peace; democracy, and stability of the whole of the Sahara region.

All of us found it emotionally very hard to deal with this downturn. Seeing the support we still had from so many people, and the determination we had to carry on. Yet being denied the right to represent the Tuaregs. As their voice, speaking to each other, and the rest of the world. Toumast had given fresh hope to so many, and it had created change. Notably a desire for the integration of the Tuareg people. Toumast had called for peace, and stability, through our music and culture. Also in the history of the Tenere we shared, and loved. Tuaregs could unite around this idea. Not because of any hatred, or racism. We saw it as a way to move forward again, as one nation.

The added bonus was that we had also made a start on reviving our culture; its language; traditions, and rituals. The stories; myths, and songs that belonged to us as a nation. It had caused us to remember our roots; the connection we had to each other, and the land we loved. For the many Tuaregs who had been displaced, Toumast was a means of giving them back this connection, and the understanding of what it meant to belong to one another, again as a nation.

Given all that has happened to my people across the years, we have learned to be resilient. So I am not prepared to say here that Toumast will never broadcast again. I am certain that it will return, and this time, as a greater and even more influential media channel than its original version. Especially since it has become even more important now for all of us to keep our hope alive, and look forward to a much brighter future.

Chapter 12

Looking To The Future Of Azawad

Although you have reached the final chapter in this book, it is not the end of the Tuaregs' story. I could have written so much more about what has already happened. The part the United States played in Malian politics. How the French don't have any gold mines of their own. Yet have accumulated more gold than any other nation. The thirteen year old girl who was captured by the jihadists when they occupied Tinbuktu a few years ago, and destroyed our heritage buildings and artifacts. The young man whose hand was cut off with a knife by Malian soldiers during one of the rebellions. For no particular reason, other than he was a Tuareg. Those who were beheaded; shot, or disabled. What has happened to so many because of their ethnicity, and colour. Being lighter or darker skinned than their assailants. The men and women who have been imprisoned, and tortured. Or simply left to die in excruciating pain.

I could have told you more about this, and the thousands of others who suffered in similar ways. Perhaps even far, far worse?

Or the man who was humiliated; tied up, and left helpless on the ground. Unable to move because of the rope which bound him from head to foot. The immediate pain of his rib bones cracking and crushed, beneath the violent impact of a heavily booted soldier. Whilst immersed in thoughts of his family who were standing nearby. His wife desperately wished to hide her eyes, and at the same time, unable to completely look away for fear of not being able to do anything. Something... to stop the horror of what was happening. Even though there was nothing to be done. The terrorists had their own agenda. They wouldn't leave until they had done what they came for.

Or maybe the young man who was arrested by Algerian border security guards, and jailed for illegally crossing the so-called national border. Without papers, or identity documents, but which the same government had denied him. A similar thing happened to another young man, at the hands of the Libyan guards. Borders which had been created artificially across the young men's traditional homeland. When arbitrary lines were drawn on a map during the Berlin Conference in 1885, at the request of the French government.

These men; women, and children had a name. Like the many others who also suffered atrocities and human rights violations, I will tell you here that all of them were Tuaregs. I also can't forget the light in the beautiful, young, woman's eyes that was dying. When she realised she was about to lose her baby. All because of the violence, and trauma, she had suffered.

This is the history I listened to as a child. When my parents and family talked quietly about what had happened to one of the elders; brother; sister; uncle; aunt; cousin; friend; friend of a friend... Or simply, another Tuareg. These are the stories of our childhood. Told at a time when the essence of life should have been about growing up, healthy, and strong. Running with the other children, and playing. Not like this. Even as a young child I knew instinctively that no one, absolutely no one whoever they might be, should have to live or die like this.

The same as it is for others, the roots of my desire to help the Tuareg people run deep through these memories and those I love. The history we share. The Tenere sands of our homeland. It is difficult sometimes to try and make sense of what has happened to us. The craziness of the violence in a situation that has become highly complex. There has already been too much evil, and wrongdoing. I believe that the only way now is to look beyond the human suffering of war and terrorism, to the future. The list of violations, and atrocities, is endless.

Unless we make it so.

That has been my aim, since I made a video of the desert people years ago. The sands of the Tenere continue to bind all of us who are known as Tuaregs. Wherever we might now live. The blood of earlier generations is in our veins. The men and women who rode their camels through Tinbuktu, and beyond. They too carried the blood of those Tuaregs who came before them.

However please remember that I am only using the word, Tuareg, for ease of reference. Each of us knows deep within our hearts who we truly are. The connection we have to each other; the place where we were born, and the past. All of this lives on within our spirit. Those who try to keep this light alive today in poetry; our music, and stories. Fighting the sense of isolation many Tuaregs feel. Whether young, or old. Not believing that there are any other options left to them. Or an escape from the unbearable lives into which they have been thrown. Whilst not even understanding in many instances what has happened, because of a lack of information. Experiencing this sense of disconnection, and even loneliness.

I am asking you now to believe that the hope for peace does remain.

For all of these reasons, we also continue to be passionate about Toumast being able to broadcast again. So that the Tuareg people can see, and hear, this message in their own language. Irrespective of the death and destruction which surrounds them, there are still those in the outside world who care about what happens, and are trying their best to help. That, like myself, will do their utmost to create the change that is needed now for us to move forward. Once again as a unified nation, with an Azawad to call our home.

It is vitally important that every Tuareg man; woman, and child should be allowed to regain his or her dignity with basic human rights. And without any further delay. While we remain the strong and noble people whom our ancestors placed their hope and dreams in thousands of years ago. Maybe even loved, when they thought of the future. The trust they placed in us that we would do our best, just as they did, for the others those of us who are left continue to represent.

It may not be easy for us to be regarded by the world as one nation again, but much can be accomplished one step at a time. Especially if taken by everyone who is historically a Tuareg. Refusing to give up until it is done. This book is a call to those in the desert and beyond; and in all levels of society to join hands. In support of each other. Those who need a helping hand in keeping their hope strong. As one family. Like the older woman who carries on determined. That she will teach the younger ones drumming and singing, for as long as she is able to. Ensuring that our culture of many thousands of years will not die, but still be there for future generations. She is the Mother of the Tuareg people.

I am deeply honoured to be known as the Man of the Sahara. Someone who interacts with the different nomadic tribes in Africa, and most know me by this name through the power of the spoken word. I have talked about Azawad, and the plight of the Tuareg nation, to as many people as I could. Of different nationalities; governments, and organisations. And I will not stop doing this.

Nearly everyone in the Sahara, including the loneliest of oases, now has access to a variety of wireless stations. Even if only by portable radio. Although this has also unfortunately enabled the extremists' recruitment of unemployed youth to gather momentum in its steady expansion. With religious leaders taking advantage of the simplicity; poverty, and ignorance of many Tuareg nomads. As well as the relatively settled people of the Sahel. Western governments and their allies have also given millions to the governments of this region. To help them fight back, in what has frequently been a vain attempt to stop radical groups from expanding their spheres of influence. Huge quantities of weapons have been deployed at astronomical cost to financially stretched governments.

When the truth of the matter is that military methods of addressing this form of radicalism haven't worked, but I believe that there is still an answer. By aiming to severely limit the future growth of terrorism. Again, through the power of the spoken word. Much better quality information, and education generally, can raise awareness about the acute dangers to which our vulnerable young people are now exposed. The one way we can realistically hope to reach: influence; inform, and educate these young men and women is through the power of the media.

We will not stop appealing to governments; governmental organisations, and NGOs to launch at least one TV station in the Tamacheq language; Arabic, and French. However modest it might be initially, its influence and effect would far outweigh this. It is necessary to act now, before it is too late. The BBC World Service; BBC Africa Radio; France24; Russia Today; the Voice of America, and others already provide channels in different languages. Including Arabic; Kurdish; Hausa, and many others. There isn't a good reason why at least one programme in the Tuareg Tamacheq (Berber) language cannot also be broadcast.

Like so many other Tuaregs I have devoted my life to ensuring that the violence and inhumanity towards our people can no longer continue. Quite simply, because I believe that this is possible, and I am a man of my people. Those who belong with the Tenere sand beneath our feet, and rightly seek to enjoy the freedom of walking there again. In peace, and without fear.

Many, many blessings to all who still seek Azawad. Hope remains, if we allow it to. As the torch which all of us can carry into the world, and the fire from which the struggle for our independence was kindled. This hope, and love, is still there. However our human rights; physical bodies, and thoughts may have been violated.

Just as our Ancestors did when they journeyed far on camels across the Sahara and found Tinbuktu, we also have the ability to create the change that is now so desperately needed.

Author's Note

I began writing this book as a factual account of what happened to the Tuaregs. Here are some of the resources I used in telling their story, if you want to look them up.

1. https://vimeo.com/user8799383
2. https://imuhagh.org
3. Baz Lecocq :
https://openaccess.leidenuniv.nl/bitstream/handle/1887/18540/ASC-075287668-2887-01.pdf
4. Jeremey Keenan:
https://newint.org/features/2012/12/01/us-terrorism-sahara

If you would like to help support the Tuaregs' cause or contact me, my email address is:

aklishekka@gmail.com

You can also send me a message on the following sites:

https://www.facebook.com/amacharoudj.akli

http://tenerevoice.blogspot.com/

Thank you for reading my book, Man Of The Sahara.

With many blessings,

Akli

Lightning Source UK Ltd.
Milton Keynes UK
UKHW042250100221
378576UK00003B/47

9 781800 314665